What people are saying about
The Truth About Money Lies...

This is not your typical book on finances. It is a book about life's experiences and what God has to say about how to handle them. In the process you will learn how to manage difficult financial decisions. This book is well worth your time.

MARK RICHT, head football coach,
University of Georgia

Russ Crosson and Kelly Talamo do a great job of joining Kelly's real-life experiences with Russ's 30-plus years of financial consulting. This book is not a financial "how-to," but rather a captivating comparison between the traditional view of money and God's view.

ANDY STANLEY, senior pastor,
North Point Community Church

Russ Crosson's *The Truth About Money Lies* is filled with stories of everyday financial situations so many of us face, coupled with strategies for surviving those financial challenges with ease. The principles he uses to help guide financial decision making are all biblically based and have withstood the test of time. As with so many challenges in life that often seem daunting, the answers can be easily found by adhering to basic Christian principles and avoiding the financial traps and lures of our modern world.

JENNY SANFORD, author and former
first lady of South Carolina

It is not hard for me to write an endorsement for *The Truth About Money Lies*. What is difficult is to keep it short. I was privileged to introduce Russ Crosson into the Christian financial planning world over 30 years ago when neither one of us knew much. I can say with certainty that Russ knows truth and is committed to truth. He has advised and counseled multitudes of people through his speaking and writing with biblical truth. He walks his talk, and this book is a compilation of many of his personal encounters with people who follow lies without even knowing it. This book is well-written, enjoyable to read, and potentially life changing. You owe it to yourself to read it for encouragement and conviction. My prayer is that you would then pass it on to the many people you influence.

RON BLUE, founder, Ronald Blue & Co., and
president, Kingdom Advisors

If you are like me, Russ Crosson is a man you'd like to spend a day with...seeking wisdom about what he's learned from the Scriptures about how to handle money and asking him to mentor you about the lies of the culture when it comes to finances. That may not be possible for you or me, but I've got the next best thing in my hands—Russ's brand-new book, *The Truth About Money Lies*. Birthed out of more than three decades of experience, Russ knows how to communicate, coach, and equip us to get it right. In these challenging economic times I want the very finest counsel and advice I can get. Buy this book and you've got it!

Russ Crosson and Kelly Talamo have chosen to cleverly present 15 life stories that demonstrate how easily and unknowingly we can fall for the world's lies about money. Yet we're not just left there. They then give sound, biblical counsel that will keep us from those traps. Whether you're newly married, about to retire, or anywhere in between, this very readable book will prove to be a valuable reminder of who really is both the source and the truth regarding your money.

I know very few people who are as qualified and effective as Russ Crosson in giving biblical, practical insight about money and life. He has given us the gift of his discernment and wisdom in *The Truth About Money Lies.* I love the straightforward, insightful way in which he addresses some of our most common misconceptions and assumptions about money. This well-written, engaging book is a priceless gift to all of us. Karen and I just wish he had written it 40 years ago!

Over the years as a newsletter publisher, I have received countless letters from my readers asking my advice on how to remedy the financial mistakes they have made. This book, through the use of real-life stories illustrating the financial lies we all are tempted with, offers biblical truths that will serve to counteract the false information about money we receive from the world. Highly recommended!

Managing our personal finances today is like tiptoeing through a minefield. Every business deal seems to come wrapped in a nice veneer, but how can we be sure? We long for a trustworthy guide to advise us about what—and what not—to do. And we want to hear it in plain, understandable language.

With the impeccable reputation of Ronald Blue & Co., CEO Russ Crosson steps up courageously to tell it like it is in our society where dollars determine the framework of our lives. He walks his readers through the process of how to read the financial compass and how to decide when to say yes and when to back off. Here is a must-have volume of rare wisdom for immediate use.

I have known Russ for over two decades and can testify that he knows the truth about money. This refreshing new treatment of age-old financial truths is a fun read…one you and your children will both enjoy.

HOWARD DAYTON, *founder,*
Compass–Finances God's Way

The Truth About Money Lies is a happy melding of the skills of two very practical thinkers. I was delighted to hear that Russ Crosson was collaborating with Kelly Talamo on this manuscript because I knew it would integrate Russ's depth of insight on money matters with Kelly's rich storytelling abilities and resources on the truth about lies. The result is evident in each chapter with its engaging story, its clear warnings, and its real-life applications that are solidly based on biblical truth.

KENNETH BOA, *president,*
Reflections Ministries, Atlanta, GA

There is probably no one in the country who understands better than Russ Crosson the "truth" about the many "money lies" that Satan has injected into the lives of people at all levels of wealth. These "lies" are insidious, pervasive in our culture, and very hard for even the Christian to recognize. This book will be an eye-opener for the unsuspecting, and should especially be put into the hands of our younger generation—from the college student to the newly married.

TERRY PARKER, *founder and board member,*
National Christian Foundation

The world screams at us its values about money. This book gives you a great opportunity to sit down and look at God's views in a fun and challenging way. We all see people every day who are suffering because they believed "money lies."

JIM REESE, *president/CEO,*
Atlanta Mission

I have read many, many books on personal finances. This one is refreshingly different. It really gets to the heart of the worldly deceptions that lead so many people astray.

BUCK MCCABE, *CFO,*
Chick-fil-A, Inc.

The Truth About
MONEY
LIES

The Truth About
MONEY LIES

RUSS CROSSON
WITH KELLY TALAMO

HARVEST HOUSE PUBLISHERS

EUGENE, OREGON

Cover by Koechel Peterson & Associates, Inc., Minneapolis, Minnesota

Published in association with the literary agency of Wolgemuth & Associates.

Harvest House Publishers has made every effort to trace the ownership of all poems and quotes. In the event of a question arising from the use of a poem or quote, we regret any error made and will be pleased to make the necessary correction in future editions of this book.

THE TRUTH ABOUT MONEY LIES
Copyright © 2012 by Russell D. Crosson
Published by Harvest House Publishers
Eugene, Oregon 97402
www.harvesthousepublishers.com

Library of Congress Cataloging-in-Publication Data
Crosson, Russ.
The truth about money lies / Russ Crosson with Kelly Talamo.
p. cm.
ISBN 978-0-7369-4545-5 (pbk.)
ISBN 978-0-7369-4546-2 (eBook)
1. Finance, Personal—Religious aspects—Christianity. I. Talamo, Kelly, 1952- II. Title.
HG179.C755 2012
332.024—dc23

2011021816

CONTENTS

ACKNOWLEDGMENTS

This book would not be possible without the contributions of many people. After I blended the truth about money lies with Kelly's stories, my longtime partner, Scott Houser, reviewed each chapter. This book would not read nearly as well without his keen eye for detail and editorial prowess. I owe him a debt of gratitude for this finished product and for putting up with my constant demands as the deadline grew near.

As with any undertaking like this, many others were involved to bring it to successful completion. My longtime assistant, Bonnie Davidson, typed and retyped more chapters than she cares to remember, and she always did it with great skill and professionalism. She deserves special commendation for handling this project along with her normal workload. I'm also grateful for Molly Blass who typed several chapters by deciphering my bad writing, and Malissa Light, who coordinated the multitude of details required when publishing a book.

A special thanks to Clark and Holly Crosson, Reed and Kristen Crosson, and Chad Crosson for reading select chapters and giving me the hope that this book would indeed communicate in a new and fresh way to all generations.

Also thanks to Bob Hawkins Jr. at Harvest House for believing in this book and encouraging us to write it.

I also owe a debt of gratitude to my partners at Ronald Blue & Co. Without their continued outstanding service to our clients and application of the truth about money, I would have a hollow platform from which to share. Kudos to my leadership team—of Brian Shepler, Vince Birley, Deborah Kimery, and Patty Warren—for picking up the slack while I focused on this book. Without their leadership skills, I would not have been able to focus on writing.

I am thankful to Julie, my wife for more than 30 years. Not only was she a constant source of encouragement and support for this book, but she has been that to me during all of my years at Ronald Blue & Co. Without her I would have nothing to say. (She also is a candid, hard editor! When her red pen came out as she reviewed the chapters, I knew the book got better and easier to understand.)

Finally I am grateful to God for giving us the Book from which all truth comes. Without His work in my life there would be no wisdom. Without His Word of truth, there would be no content for this book. To Him be the glory!!

FOREWORD

by Dan T. Cathy

As a lifelong student of God's Word and the timeless lessons and truths it contains for daily living, I was thrilled when Russ asked me to write the foreword to his new book. This is a well-timed and much-needed antidote to the many financial ills that impact today's society. And all of us need biblical reminders from time to time about how we should live, work, play, and even spend our money...wisely.

As a restaurateur, I often receive notices from the United States Treasury Department warning retailers about counterfeit bills. The updates give examples of "fake money"—as well as authentic Federal Reserve Notes—and then provide various discrepancies to look for during transactions. They are good reminders, and I always learn something meaningful from comparing the truth to lies.

You know, all of us are susceptible to falling for the world's way of making choices about our money. But biblical truths and principles are the same for all generations. They are *always* true, *always* relevant, and *always* pointing us in the direction we need to be headed. That's what this book can do for you. As we chase down different paths to find what's real about money in our daily lives, Russ shares *truth* that will ensure we are headed in the right direction financially.

And you can have confidence that Russ knows what he writes in this book. I have not only seen these truths proven in my life, but I now have the privilege of seeing them work in the lives of my children as Russ coaches and encourages them in his role of trusted financial advisor to the Cathy family.

So let me encourage you to not only enjoy this easy-to-read, story-filled book, but to have the courage to go against the grain of the world and apply these financial truths to your personal money decisions. You—and those around you—will never regret implementing truth in your financial life.

God bless, and remember to please...*eat more chicken!*

Dan T. Cathy, president and COO,
Chick-fil-A, Inc.

INTRODUCTION

Everyone picks up a book for a reason. It could be to learn, laugh, engage, or escape. But behind any of these reasons is a desire for change. We want something about ourselves to be different when we put the book down. So when we pick up a book, we say to the writer, "Teach me something I don't know or take me somewhere I've never been." Those are certainly our goals with *The Truth About Money Lies*.

It has been a joy to collaborate with Kelly Talamo on this book. For the past 20 years he has pioneered the lie/truth concept through his Men Step Up ministry. His sense of humor and story writing style set the perfect stage for my job of writing the truth component of each chapter. Even though Kelly and I have completely different gifts and very different audiences, the two of us share one thing in common: We know it's not what *we* think about money but what God thinks that matters. Therefore, we take people where they can find truth and let them decide for themselves what they should do. And that's exactly the place we would like to take you.

Welcome to *The Truth About Money Lies,* a book we believe will take you somewhere. Before we dive into this story-filled journey, we want to put your mind at ease. *This is not a "do this" book on how to manage your money.* We won't tell you how to budget, tithe, or complete an estate plan. In fact, you don't have to fill out a single worksheet. And if you don't like being told what to do (especially with your money), this book is for you. Feeling better?

How Does This Book Work?

At the beginning of each chapter, we'll tell you a story that happens every day. Each story illustrates a lie about money. There's nothing magical about the stories; they simply reveal the way people tend to think. Whenever our minds buy into a lie about money, it's just a matter of time before we live out that lie.

As you read each story, you will do what you always do. Without even thinking about it, you'll find your place, or where you fit, in the story. We'll never tell you where it is. We won't have to. If you're in the story, you'll know it as soon as you see it.

Since every truth will become evident, an application will be easy to make. At the end of each story ask yourself one of these questions: "Is this a lie I have believed?" or "Is this a lie I'm living out?" Maybe it is; maybe it isn't. We don't know. But if you're honest with yourself, *you* will know. And really, that's what matters.

After each story, we'll look at a *specific truth* that counteracts the *lie* in the story. The story illustrates how the *world* thinks about money. God's Word tells us how *He* thinks. You then get to choose how you want to think and subsequently live. It's really as simple as that.

Why will this book work for you? Every spiritual problem you and I have can be traced back to a lie we bought into. When Jesus said, "You will know the truth, and the truth will make you free" (John 8:32), He didn't mean that knowing generic truth would set us generically free from every deception that exists. Jesus meant that a *specific truth* has the power to set us free from a *specific lie* that may have us deceived. And when it comes to money, there are hundreds of them.

Here's a vivid example relating to this book. Are you ready?

> THE LIE: "We need another book about financial stewardship."
>
> THE TRUTH: "There is nothing new under the sun" (Ecclesiastes 1:9).

We never needed a book on financial stewardship—ever! In fact, we never needed a book on life, purpose, marriage, parenting, work, or money. God has already given us everything we need to know about each of those topics. It's always been right there in His Word. Take a look at the truth! "His divine power has granted us everything pertaining to life and godliness, through the true knowledge of Him who called us by His own glory and excellence" (2 Peter 1:3).

Think about it this way. If we were going to tell you the truth about how to manage your money, where would we get it? We would have to go to the same place Ronald Blue, Larry Burkett, and every other man and woman of God interested in financial truths go—the Scriptures.

Neither Kelly nor I claim to be prophets, but we can make you one huge promise. If you'll apply truth to any lie you believe, you will never wind up living that lie. And that's a gold nugget you can take to the bank! So, enjoy your time with us as we explore financial truth.

1

Truth Defined

Before we look at some of the common lies about money and how they impact our lives, it's critical that we unpack the concept of truth.

What is truth? Truth is that which is fact, a reality that's certain, genuine, correct, and immovable. It's honest, solid, and never artificial. It never changes. It is the same yesterday, today, and forever.

Where does truth come from? This is where it gets interesting. At first glance there appear to be hundreds, if not thousands, of "truth sources" to choose from. But in reality there are only two that we can look to: the world and God's Word, the Bible. Both will shape our thinking. One will conform us to a system where we'll think and act like everyone else. The other will renew our minds and empower us to think and act like children of God.

The cold, chilling truth is that when it comes to our money, many of us choose to get our truth (facts and reality) from the world. And that shouldn't surprise us. After all, we're inundated by the world's way of thinking through a constant media bombardment, including Twitter, iPhones, iPads, laptops, magazines, news shows, and

500-plus cable channels on every topic imaginable. Media sound bites, regardless of their source, accuracy, or validity end up defining reality for us. Often we don't even take time to check out the source of a media "fact." Is it reliable? Is it accurate? Have I checked this against any other source? As more and more of our "facts" come from media, is it any wonder that our framework for thinking is being influenced by the world? And this is especially true about money issues.

What do media voices tell us about money? That we only go around once so take on debt and buy whatever you want. Live your life with the gusto you deserve. The world says work is bad (TGIF), so hurry up and earn a bundle so you can quit working, retire, and enjoy life. The world says taxes are a problem and budgets are restrictive. We're bombarded with the "fact" that it's okay to overspend because we can always pay off debt with cheaper dollars later. Keep money close to the vest and never talk about it. Make sure we leave our children a big pile of money so they don't have to go through what we went through. On top of all of this, we're never encouraged to give our money away to good causes. Instead we're told that our next purchase will bring us happiness.

> Truth-based decisions ultimately
> produce the best results.

It's our contention, however, that in order to experience absolute freedom, especially in the area of money, it's imperative that we get our truth from God's Word. Jesus said to God, "Your word is truth" (John 17:17). The apostle Paul told us that God cannot lie (Titus 1:2). And David put it all so well when he told the Lord, "The sum of Your word is truth" (Psalm 119:160). If we take the

Word of God and add it all up, it amounts to absolute truth! In light of that, wouldn't it be wise for us to get our facts and reality about life from the God of the universe? From the One who cannot tell a lie and who offers us the truth to live by through His Word?

We all have a system of beliefs (a "truth system," if you will) that affects every decision we make. That truth system is either built on what comes from the world or what comes from God's Word. There's no middle ground. And what we believe will always play out in the way we live. Let us illustrate.

The world has little or no fear of being in debt. For decades the world has told us that the way to get ahead is to borrow. In other words, use other people's money to get what we want. But the Bible (truth from God's Word) flatly contradicts that. It says the borrower becomes the lender's (the master's) slave. As long as we're able to make our payments, everything seems fine because the master is quiet. But the truth is that we're really in bondage. And the moment we can't pay, the master calls in his chips. With the present rash of mortgage foreclosures and the increase in personal bankruptcies, we're seeing the impact of the bondage of debt as tens of thousands of families feel the exacting hand of their debt masters.

I (Russ) have been in the financial business 30 years, and I've noticed an interesting shift. It used to be when people were asked if they had debt they would say, "No—except, of course, my home mortgage." Now they say "no" even while having multiple mortgages, auto loans, and typically owe on a credit card or two. *How can that be?* Did the definition of debt suddenly change? No, but *perception* has changed. We have regressed so far in our thinking that we no longer call "debt" debt!

The world says, "Everybody has a home mortgage so that's not really debt. Everybody has a car loan so that's not really debt. We can make the payments so we're okay." But our interpretation of debt doesn't change the facts. We, the borrowers, are still slaves to the lenders.

We know intuitively that truth-based decisions ultimately produce the best results. But truth-based decisions often appear to be "no fun" in light of many competing alternatives. And who wants that? Who wants to take the fun out of life? I would really enjoy a (new car, new computer, new boat, vacation, bigger house) now, so why not get it right now? The answer is "Don't do it." Why? Because *decisions based on truth will ultimately allow us to experience peace of mind and abundant life:* Jesus said, "I came that [you] may have life, and have it abundantly" (John 10:10).

Few of us would place more value on "fun" than on "peace of mind," but we make our decisions quite to the contrary. We make some of our decisions based on flat-out lies, even when deep down in our hearts we know better. And this is especially true in the area of finances.

We are free to accept or reject the truth. We are just not free from the consequences.

It's no accident that the New Testament focuses so much on financial matters. Believing a worldly lie about money clouds our minds to the truths in God's Word. It takes our focus from our eternal God and places it on temporal things. And it shifts our affections from the God who loves us to that which has no lasting value.

There's one more problem with financial lies. Financial lies can take a long time to recover from. We can get into debt overnight, but it will take years to get out of it. One swipe of a credit card can be a five-year setback, and one bad investment can take a lifetime to right. The first half of John 10:10 describes Satan's true role in preventing abundant life: "The thief comes only to steal and kill and destroy." Have any lies in the financial area of your life destroyed any abundance in the life you now live? Of course they have. That's their purpose. That's what they do.

When it comes to learning the truth and avoiding lies about money, it's wise that we prepare for battle. We're up against some very formidable opposition. First John 2:16 says, "All that is in the world, the lust of the flesh and the lust of the eyes and the boastful pride of life, is not from the Father, but is from the world." In addition to the world, our very own flesh is working against us. This is why it's so important to understand the truth from God's Word. Only *His truth* will set us free.

Feeling overwhelmed? Don't be. That same Word full of truth tells us, "Greater is He who is in you than he who is in the world" (1 John 4:4). God has made it clear that for every lie that ensnares us, there's a corresponding truth to set us free. God has made His Word clear and simple! So, in keeping with our lie/truth theme:

THE LIE: "There are unlimited uses of money."

THE TRUTH: "At the end of the day, any-thing you do with your money will fit into one of five categories."

I know you're probably thinking that's crazy. There's got to be a lot more than that, right? No. Every credit card swipe, every check, every use of cash, every dollar that flows from your hands will fall into one of these five categories:

- Living or lifestyle expenses
- Charitable giving
- Income taxes

- Debt repayment
- Savings or investments

And guess what? The great deceiver produces lies for each of these categories! And if he decided to take a vacation, the lies wouldn't disappear. We're perfectly capable of making them up ourselves. In fact, as long as we're breathing, we can lie to ourselves about how we use our money.

Over the next several chapters we'll unpack the most pervasive lies in those five areas. Our format is simple. We'll tell a story, identify the lie, and then state the truth from God's Word. Your application of God's truth is what will set you free.

So how about it? Are you ready for the truth about money lies? Remember, you are free to accept or reject the truth. You are not free from the consequences if you choose to reject truth. Choose wisely and freedom awaits!

2

STRETCHED OUT

Six years of clipping coupons, driving clunkers, and making do with a 900-square-foot home was about to pay off for Mark and Jill Thompson. They were ready to move into a larger house and start a family. It's something they had prayed and saved for since the day they were married.

Hearing the Thompsons were in the market to buy a house, Tom, an acquaintance from church, suggested they use his mortgage broker. "Listen, Mark, if there's any guy in town who can get your deal done, Jay Stafford's the man," Tom touted. "Jay helped Lisa and me get more home than we imagined with a smaller note than we dreamed. And the way prices are climbing in our area, we could flip our home today and walk away with a $30,000 profit."

"Wow!" Mark replied. "You said $30,000 profit in less than a year? That's impressive."

"I'm telling you, brother, Jay is the wizard!" Tom continued. "The guy knows financing like our minister knows the Bible. He's amazing! You'll see. Here's what you do. You and Jill go downtown and meet with Jay. Tell him what you're looking for and how much you can spend. And on that note, keep an open mind. He can teach you guys a lot. He really opened our eyes about financing. Once you decide on your price point, Jay can give you an approval letter that you can take with you house shopping. That's what we did. Once we found what we wanted, we showed the builder what we were approved for. It was like waving money at the guy. He jumped at our offer. Trust me, Mark, you guys will be out of your cracker box before you know it. Just say the word, and I'll set you guys up."

"Thanks, Tom!" Mark responded. "That sounds great. If you don't mind setting it up, we'd love to meet with Jay. I'm off on Tuesdays. Is that enough notice?"

"Knowing Jay, that's plenty. I'll let him know, and he'll call you to confirm it."

Two days later the Thompsons were on the fifteenth floor of the Piedmont Building waiting for Jay to make his entrance. His impressive office included a huge mahogany table, some thick leather chairs, and a killer view. But the scene wasn't nearly as impressive as the sharply dressed broker himself. He arrived right on time. With incredible passion and pinpoint accuracy, he laid out three income-based scenarios for Mark and Jill. He showed them what they could get, how much to put down, and exactly what it would cost them per month. He even had a "bonus" column showing a way to pay their home off more quickly. The guy was exceeding all expectations. And when Mark glanced at Jill and gave her a huge thumbs-up, she knew right then that he was hooked. But she remained a little hesitant.

Jill fidgeted nervously as the broker ran through current interest rates and possible options. He was clearly in his element and barely paused to take a breath. *This guy's good,* she thought. *He knows numbers like the back of his hand. He's everything Tom said he would be. But something is not right. This isn't what I had in mind at all. In fact, it's not even close. We should walk out that door this very minute.*

Every effort Jill made to get Mark's attention proved to be an act of futility. He and Jay were so locked in it was as if she weren't even in the room. The more they talked, the more anxious she became. Eventually Jill felt on the verge of getting sick.

"That's the way I see it, Mark," Jay said emphatically. "You guys have pinched pennies long enough. Now it's time to let your money work for you. With this new product I can lock you in at 3 percent with a point a year rise for the next five years. And you only need to put down half the money you've saved up."

"Wow! That sounds great, Jay. Jill and I were looking at houses in the mid $200,000s. Are you saying we'd qualify for more than that?"

"Mark, with your credit rating and this product, you left that neighborhood way behind. You qualify for closer to $400,000, which could land you guys on the north side of town. I'll give you a letter to that effect, and you can start shopping for whatever you want. I know you said you plan on living where you are a while, but the way this market is climbing, you could make a killing long before the adjustable rate mortgage matures."

Unable to hold her tongue any longer, Jill nervously blurted, "Wait a minute, Jay. Mark and I didn't plan on spending anywhere near that much money."

"That's the beauty of this, Jill. You wouldn't be!" Jay said. "You can take the $15,000 that you don't put down and invest it in the market. The market typically earns 4 to 6 percent more than what you would pay on the mortgage. Think about that. You'll be *making* more money on the principal that you don't have to put down on the house. Sure, you might have to stretch a little, but that's how you get ahead. The bottom line is that you'll get way more house for a lot less money down. All the while, your home is working for you. That's one of the reasons they call your home your biggest asset."

"I don't know…" Jill looked to Mark for support. "This is not at all what we talked about. What happened to just getting a little nicer home with a bit more room for the family? Isn't that what we've been planning and saving for?"

"Yes," Mark responded. "And this way we can do that *and* make some money as well. We can't pass up an opportunity like this, Jill. This doesn't come along every day. This is like a gift!"

"Mark, that's more house to furnish, insure, and take care of! Not to mention the north side is Jackson County. Aren't the taxes much higher in Jackson County?"

"She's right about that one, Mark," Jay agreed. "Jackson County taxes are a little higher, but it also has the best school system in the state. And since you'll be raising a family, you need to consider schools. That's a game changer for most couples."

"I didn't know that," Mark admitted. "That's something we need to consider, Jill."

"Of course it's something to consider. Everything is something to consider," Jill said emphatically. "And right now, Mark, I'm considering the debt. We're about to go down to one income, remember? What if something happens to you or your job? How do we make double the payments we've been making and raise a family if something were to happen? How would we do that? The bottom line is I don't have peace about this idea. That's way more debt than we've ever had!"

"Look, Jill," Mark responded, "I know it looks a little scary, and I totally understand how you feel. But let's keep one thing in mind, okay? If we get too stressed or money gets too tight, we'll just downsize a bit."

𝕁𝕃

Did you catch the error?

> **The Lie:** "If things get tight, we can always sell and get out of debt."

Countless couples live inside the tension the Thompsons felt that day. Many of us have straddled the fence while a sharp broker or salesperson tried to sway us. It's hard to think we've been thinking too small. It's no fun to be told to abandon your dreams or to be told you don't dream big enough. It's gut-wrenching.

Is stretching for more the right thing to do? Is qualifying for a bigger loan really a "gift"? Are low interest rates and limited-time offers really opportunities we can't afford to miss? There's a very fine line between faith and presumption, and it's a line we don't want to cross. On one side is good stewardship; the other side is greed. That's why we need to ask those questions. We also need to ask these:

- "Should I enter this agreement?"
- "What will happen if I can't pay this debt?"
- "Is any of my thinking or planning based on presumption?"
- "Why should I listen to this person's counsel?"

As hard as these questions may seem, the consequences of ignoring them are far worse. The good news is we don't have to guess at the answers. God answers them for us.

> THE TRUTH: "Don't be one of those who enter agreements, who put up security for loans. If you have no money to pay, even your bed will be taken from under you" (Proverbs 22:26-27 HCSB).

God knows the way we think. He's well aware that we seldom (if ever) borrow money while thinking about the worst that can happen. For us, a loan is a means to get what we want when we want it. That precludes us from thinking through all that could go wrong. Seldom do we allow ourselves to imagine the worst-case scenario of our actions. If we did, we probably wouldn't borrow… at least not as much as we do.

And that's what Jay did. He had Mark thinking only about the positives. And once Mark saw Jay's point of view, he couldn't see Jill's. Or he didn't want to. He didn't want to think about the negatives.

In addition to being blinded by what we want when we want it, none of us likes to be told what (or what not) to do. We didn't like it from our parents or teachers. We don't like to hear it from our spouses. And we don't even like to hear it from God! We feel like we might miss out. So instead of giving us a negative command, God gives us two very vivid scenarios that paint a picture of where our actions could take us.

The first illustration reveals what happens when we can't pay a debt. The modern-day terms are *foreclosure* and *repossession*. And that's exactly what Jill was trying to get at. If Jill wasn't making her thoughts clear, the same cannot be said about God. He is *very* clear! "If you have no money to pay, even your bed will be taken from under you" (Proverbs 22:27 HCSB). He doesn't just say we'll lose all our stuff. He pinpoints a very specific loss. He points out that *we could lose our beds.* Really? Our beds? Is God prohibiting furniture loans here?

Well, yes and no. The bed itself is half the point. There's a much greater loss that God wants us to consider. What is the most private area of your home? Where do you snuggle with your spouse and talk about kids? Where do you lay your head down to rest? Where do you dream? God is saying that before you borrow think about this: When you can't pay your bills, even this last bastion of peace will be taken from you. Every dream will be wiped out. You'll be in a place where there is no rest.

Proverbs 13:10 is also clear: "Arrogance [presumption] leads to nothing but strife, but wisdom is with those who receive counsel."

This discusses "presumptive possession" instead of repossession. The focus is on what we *can get* instead of what we can lose. We can get strife if we overreach what is prudent. And when we get counsel, we need to make sure it's biblically based.

Think back on our story and notice how much of Jay's outcomes were rooted in presumption:

- The housing market will continue to go up.
- You will be able to flip this house.
- Money in the market will always outperform the interest you're paying.

And when Jill pushed Mark for an answer to a worst-case scenario, his response was loaded with much of the same:

- "If things get tight, we can always sell and get out of debt."

Here's the problem with presumption. It's *conjecture*. It presupposes something will happen that we really have no control over. What's deadly is that presumption is an *inner belief*. That's why it looks so much like faith. We really believe it. In order to distinguish the two, it's important to note *the object* of faith. Biblical faith is rooted in what *God can do*. Presumption is typically rooted in what is *historically* true.

> Wisdom is the application of
> knowledge (facts) in a practical,
> biblical, and successful way.

Some presumptions may have worked in the past, but the challenge is that we need to plan for potential outcomes and worst-case scenarios. We need to remember that everything is cyclical, and even though something may have worked in the past, it may not work in the future (Ecclesiastes 3:1-8; James 4:13-16). Presumption can cause incredible strife!

The antidote for presumption is found in the second half of Proverbs 13:10: "Wisdom is with those who receive counsel." *Talk* to people who believe in the Bible and who have been where you're going. We need to have somebody wise in God's Word and in money matters to help us check our thinking and ask if we're being presumptive. By asking for advice, we don't lose a thing. In fact, we get to possess something that's a lot more precious than whatever we're chasing: *Wisdom!*

Wisdom is the application of knowledge (facts) in a practical, biblical, and successful way. So what knowledge do we have about this house decision? First, we know we're capable of convincing ourselves of anything, especially in the financial arena. This is why we need wise, biblically based counsel in areas where we should mistrust our judgment. And a house-buying decision is primary among them.

Too much house too soon will
keep our finances on edge.

Second, we know that a house-buying decision is likely one of the most critical decisions we'll make relative to our finances.

Third, we know that everything moves in cycles, and this needs to be factored in.

Too much house too soon will keep our finances on edge. Simple logic tells us that the bigger the house, the greater the upkeep and the more the furnishings cost. This will add stress to the budget. Jill's warning to Mark was right on point.

As I've counseled individuals over the years, I have found several reasons why people buy too much house too soon:

- *Fearing we might miss a "really great deal."* This was certainly Mark's thought. As long as I have been in this business, I've yet to see the last "great deal." In fact, I bet someone will call me next week with a "can't miss" opportunity. We should decide how much house we can afford within our budget, and then stay at that level.

  Julie and I experienced this when we bought our first house. We were incredibly excited to find a home that was in foreclosure and owned by the bank in a neighborhood of $110,000 homes. The bank wanted $85,000 for the house, but when we went through our budget, we determined we could only afford to pay $80,000. This would allow us to put 20 percent down and comfortably afford the payments on the mortgage. The additional $5000 on the mortgage would have stretched our budget.

  We had a choice to make. We could either "stretch" (the all-American way) or determine we were going to trust God and stay with what we had planned. I remember vividly sitting on the couch and telling Julie we weren't going to just say we trusted God, we were going to actively trust Him.

  We made the decision not to buy the house (even though it was a good deal) and went back to looking in the newspaper for houses again. It wasn't 10 minutes after we made our decision that the phone rang and the price of the house had been dropped the additional $5000—down to the $80,000 that we had committed to spend. That was the price we needed to make the budget work. *Incredible!* Julie and I clearly saw God's hand at work. When we jump in and borrow instead of waiting on God, we often miss seeing and experiencing His solutions.

- *Believing that personal income will always go up.* Since a home mortgage and the upkeep on a house are typically our largest budget items, it can be devastating when our income takes a dive. We certainly observe this firsthand during economic downturns and high unemployment levels. I always encourage my clients to build a cushion into their budget. And the best way to do this is to never buy too much house too soon. A cushion also makes it easier to live on one income if necessary. Jill tried to remind Mark of this reality.

- *Trying to maintain a certain standard of living.* Many times people buy too much house because they want to have a house like they grew up in. What they forget is their parents may have worked 30 years to have that house. There is a reason we use the term "starter homes." It's a home that's designed for one to start out in, but with the view of only staying there the minimum amount of time it takes to *safely* move up to the longer-term, "bigger" house.

  Unfortunately many people don't stay in their starter homes quite long enough. There's something in us that wants to "move up." But moving up is what keeps finances on edge. One thing I learned after a trip to Africa years ago is that people can't buy a starter hut! Over there it is called *shelter*. We would do well in this country to look at our homes as the shelters God intended instead of trying to keep up with the Joneses with bigger and fancier houses.

- *Losing the fear of being in debt.* As I said in the introduction, I've listened to people refuse to call a mortgage "debt." In their mind's eye, it is "just part of the deal." Everybody in America has a mortgage, right? So that's "not really" debt, is it? Unfortunately, those who have gone through an economic meltdown understand that it is indeed a debt. Countless people lose their homes because they assume that house prices and incomes always go up. They also assume that if things did get tough, they can simply sell their homes and pay off the debt. But as history has played out, people have been wrong on both counts.

It's good to maintain a healthy fear of debt.

The facts are clear. In past recessions, many people couldn't sell their houses, and many that could were selling them for much less than the debt owed. As a result, they ended up losing any equity they had, along with their place to live—not to mention their peace of mind.

What went wrong? Was it just a downturn in the economy or was it something deeper? The answer is simple: Truth was ignored. If you can't pay what you owe, the banker (your master) is sure to come calling. It's good to maintain a healthy fear of debt. Don't just look at the payments you will make, but consider the total mortgage amount that will have to be repaid at some point.

- *Houses are a good investment.* This is somewhat similar to the previous point, but from a slightly different perspective. In the post-war years, Americans came to believe that their houses were the best investment they would ever make. They mixed the investment ingredient into their need for a home. Homes are intended to be a safe place to live and raise families. The truth is that investments involve risk, and we should separate risk from our house-purchase decision as much as possible.

As a matter of fact, I encourage you to consider the house "personal property" rather than an investment. When I do clients' net worth statements, I don't show the houses they live in as investments because it's highly doubtful that any time it goes up in value they would sell it just for the investment return. A house is a place where we want to raise our families and build memories. Therefore, it should be treated as such, rather than as an investment that can be bought and sold frequently.

We all want a nice home, and I'm all for that desire! If you want to buy the best home for your money, here is my counsel. Ready? *Buy a home you really like, but insist that the home you buy allows you to experience maximum peace of mind.* Here are five tips to help you achieve that:

- *Always put at least 20 percent down.* This ensures your mortgage principal is less, reduces monthly payments, and enables you to avoid higher costs, such as mortgage insurance.

- *Strive to get a 15-year mortgage.* A shorter term mortgage forces you to put more of your money into debt repayment sooner. Yes, it could make your budget tight, but in the long run it's highly doubtful you will ever regret putting that money into principal instead of interest payments. Avoid interest-only and adjustable-rate mortgages.

- *If you cannot live in the house at least two to three years, you are better off renting a home rather than buying.* As a financial advisor, I've worked through the analysis to determine which is better—buying or renting. Factoring in mortgage payments, utilities, taxes, insurance, repairs and maintenance, closing costs, real estate commissions, and various appreciation and tax rate assumptions, it always comes out best financially to rent if you can't live in a home for more than two to three years.

  One of the greatest financial fallacies is that renting is throwing money away. That's not the case. It's really important for young couples and people just starting careers to grasp this truth. Until they're settled in their jobs, in their churches, and in the school systems for their children (knowing they are unlikely to move for a few years), it's much more freeing to rent instead of rushing out to buy and taking on more responsibility and financial risk.

Your kids do not really care where they live.

- *Live in the current house a little longer.* Resist the urge to upgrade houses for an extra year or two, and during that time put more into savings. Remember, the bigger the house the more upkeep, taxes, and other costs. Saving money for a larger down payment on the new house will pay dividends with lower monthly payments for years to come. As a matter of fact, why not save up so you can keep your mortgage payment the same as it is now?

- *Your kids do not really care where they live.* Many of us buy into the lie that what we do is for the kids. It's been Julie's and my experience that our children don't care about the house they live in as long as we're there to spend time with them. It doesn't make much sense for us to be off working harder to pay the mortgage on a bigger house and never be around for our families.

    Not convinced? Look back at your own child-hood. What memories come to you? Are you holding a grudge because your bedroom was small? Was your heart broken because your yard didn't have sprinklers? Did you cry yourself to sleep because you didn't live in a gated community? No way. The only regrets you have about growing up are probably in the relationships you did or didn't have, not in the amount of square footage that framed them.

Julie and I have never regretted being committed to these home-buying principles. We understood the truth that we'll never know what the future holds, so we committed to making our house into a home and not an albatross around our necks.

❧ THINKING IT THROUGH ❧

❏ Whether you are renting or buying, is your living situation the best one for you financially right now?

❏ Did you have a good financial foundation when you bought your first home, or did purchasing your home create unexpected stress?

❏ As you look at the five reasons people buy too much house too soon, did you fall prey to any of those? If so, which ones? If not, how did you avoid them?

❏ When you bought your home, did you consider the "peace of mind" factor? Why or why not?

❏ As you look at the five tips to gain more peace of mind when buying a home, what is the one thing you can do right now that will help you move in that direction?

3

THE COUPLE NEXT DOOR

The Watts have been married for nearly five years. They enjoy their work, have great friends at church, and are very intentional about living their faith. Life is good but far from perfect for this young Christian couple. Greg's company is downsizing, and his future there is tenuous at best. While Annie's artwork endeavor is very fulfilling, she does well to break even financially. And even though they want children, every attempt thus far has failed.

The Watts live in a part of town that has recently become trendy. Like many couples around them, they bought one of the older homes at just the right time, made some improvements, and are now enjoying a steep increase in their property value. High ceilings and wide, wooden plank floors add charm and character to older homes. They also carry a lot of noise, which usually bothers Greg when he's trying to work. But today, as Annie's singing along with the radio begins to ring through the house, he doesn't mind a bit. He smiles, glances at the clock, and shuts his laptop. His thoughts turn to the past…

Before Greg met Annie, he was a rising sales star in a software company. His high-speed mind and great personality helped make him an instant success. Extensive travel and long hours didn't bother Greg. Work was an extension of his social life, and his big commissions afforded him some expensive toys he enjoyed on weekends. From his vantage point, with his killer apartment, two cars, and a boat, things were falling right into place as he had planned. All he needed now was to find the right woman.

Greg dated a lot, but he'd never dated a woman like Annie. She was special. Annie loved to talk about what really mattered in life and wasn't afraid of topics with depth. Not only was she sensitive, but Annie also had exceptional insight. And though her natural beauty first drew Greg in, her love for Christ won him over.

Greg claimed to be a Christian; Annie lived like one. Everything she did—what she wore, what she read, how she treated people, and how she managed money—had its root in what she believed. Her life had purpose. And when Greg asked what she sought in a man, her answer cut him to the quick. "I'm looking for a man who loves God and lives by His Word!" Right there Greg decided that he'd better become that man. That decision won Annie over, and soon the two were engaged.

Greg and Annie could talk about anything. In fact, their communication was borderline stellar. The only rub came when they first sat down to work on their upcoming budget. It was a conflict that neither one saw coming, and it threated to end their engagement. The root of the problem was very simple—they had different definitions of "freedom." For Greg, freedom meant having whatever they wanted. For Annie, freedom meant having just what they needed without debt.

It's never easy to change a lifestyle, especially if it involves downsizing to a lifestyle we can afford. Cash flow can be very deceptive. While a positive cash flow can cover our bills, it can also cover a ton of mistakes—mistakes seldom seen until the veil of illusion is taken away.

Tension grew at every budget discussion. Annie would list their future monthly expenses and show how they could cut them by 40 percent. Greg would counter with their combined monthly income, citing how they could still tithe and save above what they spent. He wasn't interested in cutting a thing. Thirty days before the wedding, the stress grew into all-out war.

"Listen, Annie!" Greg shouted in frustration. "I've told you over and over. If at some point we have to sell something, we will. But it's right here on paper—*combined income of $110,000*. We can easily afford what we have. For as sharp as you are, you sure don't get finances. Do you have any idea the loss we'd take by selling my boat right now? Instead of constantly harping on what to get rid of, you should be thankful for how God has blessed us."

"Blessed us?" Annie questioned, pointing to the column of outstanding debts. "Is that what you call $1000 in monthly payments? How is all of this debt for things we don't need a blessing from God? Tell me where you got that one, Greg?"

"Funny, you didn't complain about the boat when I proposed to you on it. In fact, I think I recall hearing you say 'how blessed you were' right after I put that rock on your finger. Have you forgotten that already?" Greg asked sarcastically.

"No!" Annie said, fighting back tears. "I haven't forgotten a thing! The blessing I meant is what God has given us *together*. It has nothing to do with a boat or a ring. Don't you see that? It's about us, Greg!" And with that said, Annie broke down.

Trying to calm his fiancée down, Greg conceded. "Okay. Look, I don't want you to be upset. I love that you're so practical. And I understand how you feel about debt. You were raised that way, and I respect that. But listen, honey. I can promise you this: We'll never keep anything we can't afford. Don't worry. I have the expenses covered."

Annie saw the situation clearly. She and Greg were at a spiritual crossroads, one that would define their future relationship. This battle wasn't about their monthly expenses. This was a battle over how they would live. Leaning on what she knew to be true, Annie took a deep breath and boldly spoke up. "All income is a blessing, Greg. That's God's way of providing for us. But to use that blessing to pay on debt for things we don't even need isn't just poor stewardship, it's voluntary slavery. And slavery is no way to begin our marriage. We can't do that, Greg. And as much as I love you, I won't do that."

THE LIE: "As long as we can make the payments, we're fine."

THE TRUTH: "The rich rule over the poor, and the borrower is slave to the lender" (Proverbs 22:7 NIV).

How can two very intelligent people look at the same information and see two different things? Easy. They view it through different lenses. Greg looked at the numbers through the lens of the world; Annie through the lens of the truth in God's Word.

We can all relate to how quickly a budgeting session can burst into flames. But the problem Greg and Annie faced had little to do with the budget itself. Budgets rarely are the problem. They do, however, reveal underlying assumptions and values. Budgeting doesn't cause people to fight; it merely pinpoints their real conflict. Just like Greg and Annie, most couples' fights over money aren't about the budget at all. The real fight is over what they choose to believe.

Greg did something that's easy to do...something that most

of us do. He minimized the power of debt by citing that his cash flow was positive. Now on paper, that makes total sense. On paper we're ahead of the game. On paper we have sufficient "margin" for the extras. But our lives are never *lived* on paper. They're lived in the reality of utility bills, car repairs, unexpected expenses, medical bills, and so on.

One of the beauties of the Bible is that some of the most powerful, life-changing truths are clearly stated in just a few words. Proverbs 22:7 exemplifies that. In this short-but-powerful verse, God exposes us to an important economic principle. The first part of the verse is easy to grasp: "The rich rule over the poor." In other words, the rich are in power. I can't think of any country where a guy in a mud hut is making decisions for people in mansions. We get that. We understand the power and control that goes with having money. That's part of the reason we want it. It gives us leverage and enables us to get things, do things, and have things. And some of that isn't bad at all.

But part two of this verse is a different story. This is where we tend to get off base. As much as we might say we believe God's Word, this is where we can turn a deaf ear and allow the world to have its way. "The borrower is slave to the lender." And as hard as this might be for us to swallow, positive cash flow does not change the facts. *Behind every debt is a master waiting.* The fact that we're able to pay on time for now doesn't make the lender go away. It only makes the master a little nicer to us.

We may look "free" on paper because we have enough money to pay the bills, but in reality we're anything but. Are you having a hard time with this? Try *not* making a monthly payment and watch the lender's attitude change. Quit paying a debt and see how free you really are.

"It was for freedom that Christ set us free" (Galatians 5:1). Why do we so willingly embrace financial bondage?

Monthly Payments

Most Americans don't see "positive cash flow" as financial bondage. We can make the payments and presume we will always be able to make them, so what's the problem with that? Why should we wait for something we can have now by making just a few monthly payments? We want what we want, and we want it now. In fact, we want today what our parents were able to have only after 30 years of work. We look horizontally at our siblings, friends, neighbors, coworkers, and college classmates and feel we deserve what they have. After all, we're working hard too. So we buy it even if we can't really afford it ("afford" defined as paying cash). We do what Will Rogers said: "We spend money we don't have [borrowed money] to buy things we don't need, to impress people we don't even like." And in so doing, we live a lie and stay in financial bondage.

The world does not help us here either. Commercials bombard us with the idea that we "deserve it" or "so worldly, so welcome" (that last clever jingle advertised a credit card). Ask a car salesperson what the number one question people ask when buying a new car is and what do you think the answer will be? Right. "How much are the monthly payments?" Few buyers hone in on the *total* cost, which is the real issue. I recently received my gas bill in the mail, and in the envelope was a flyer with pictures of several different gas grills for great, warm-weather cookouts. I was intrigued to observe that nowhere in the flyer could I find the price of the grills. I saw $15.11/month, $24.78/month, $28.17/month, and so on…but no total price. And on top of that nowhere was the interest rate mentioned!

At the height of the real estate market boom, I received an imitation check in the mail from a local bank. It said they had good news for me. Due to the rising home values in my area, I qualified to "get ahead" by combining my mortgage and other debts *plus* I could get an additional $44,000 in cash. Wow! More debt will wipe out stress and allow me to get ahead!

From another bank I received an offer to buy a car with a "tax-smart" loan. This loan offered great savings, the ad said, because the interest was entirely tax deductible. To qualify, I simply needed to use my house as part of the collateral. Oh my word! Not only am I *saving money* with the loan, but I am now *smart.* To top it off, I tie my house into this, taking a productive asset (my home) to buy a consumer item.

These ads are illustrations of how the world tries to make us feel dumb by not living its way. Words such as "smart," "savings," and "getting ahead," are designed to fool us into believing money lies. And if these ads aren't bad enough, one credit card application really took the cake: "Important notice! Throw this away *only* if you like to throw away *your money.*" I was incredulous. Here is a credit card company attempting to entice me by telling me that I am throwing away my money if I do not use their card (and pay an exorbitant interest rate). And most of us receive multiple credit card applications every week! Unfortunately, many people will fall into that trap and add more and more credit cards to their wallets and purses, not realizing that the money offered so freely isn't theirs to start with.

The key to financial freedom is exhibiting *financial maturity:* forgoing present desires for future rewards and benefits.

Unfortunately, we use the ease of credit cards to immediately have things without currently paying for them—even when we know that the interest-rate terms of the cards are very high. Think about that. We live in a time when things aren't really paid for. We focus on cash flow, on making payments. We can buy almost anything with a payment plan: refrigerators, microwaves, cell phones, and so on. The problem with this is that we'll never extricate ourselves from the bondage that debt creates if we keep a mindset of "making payments."

> The truth is that borrowing today sentences
> us to a restricted lifestyle in the future.

Our impatience and willingness to fall for enticing commercials fool us into not realizing that seldom are we told the rest of the story. Debt is debt, and it must be paid back. Until it is paid back, the borrower is a slave to the lender. Just because I can make the payments doesn't mean the debt isn't there. To the contrary, if I have to make payments on a consumer item, I can't afford that item. The truth is that borrowing today sentences us to a restricted lifestyle in the future.

How long do we have to live in this restricted or lower lifestyle? Consider this: If I owe $2000 on a credit card and make only the minimum monthly payments, *it will take 32 years to pay it back!* That's right—32 years to pay it back by making minimum payments. Why? Because most of the payments are going toward interest. Although the time and cost vary with the credit card company, remember that those companies allow us to make minimum payments for a reason: It maximizes *their* profits.

My two oldest sons recently married. One truth I hope I have passed on to them is to have a healthy fear of debt (especially consumer debt). I've shared with them that the key to financial freedom is exhibiting *financial maturity: forgoing present desires for future rewards and benefits.* If they will make it harder on themselves early in their marriages by living within their incomes and doing without nonessentials, life will get easier as they get older. Why? A few important reasons. First, they will have learned the discipline of living on a budget (more on that later) and spending less than they make. Second, they will not have debt to pay off in the future, which will increase their margin, flexibility, and freedom.

Delayed Gratification

In addition to looking at the terrible financial consequences of financing our lifestyles with debt, we also need to look at the concept of *delayed gratification*. Instead of gratifying a current desire by buying it now, we need to be willing to wait.

I remember early in our marriage when Julie and I didn't have a dining room table. Oh, we could have purchased one to fill up that empty space in our dining room, but we would have missed out on some valuable experiences. First, it was a testimony to friends who came over for dinner when we had to carry our "sofa table" into the dining room and put folding chairs around it to eat. When they asked what we were doing, we shared our convictions regarding consumer debt and paying cash for depreciable items. Second, we had a greater appreciation for the nice, handmade dining room table we were able to purchase two years later for cash. Not only was it a superior product than we would have purchased on credit, but something about having to wait made us enjoy that new table all the more.

If you can't pay cash for a consumer
item, don't buy it. Wait. Save. Pay cash.

Delayed gratification isn't just a monthly payment or debt issue. It can also be an issue of priorities and keeping life in balance.

Looking back, there were times when Julie and I could have paid cash for an item we wanted, but we had higher spending goals for funds, such as building an emergency fund and saving for our kids' education. By employing the principle of delayed gratification, our financial lives stayed in better balance and we had peace of mind.

At this point, you may be wondering if debt is ever okay. All debt can create bondage and should be feared, but most to be feared is *consumer debt*. Generally, debt may make sense for items that have the *potential* to increase in value (primarily businesses and real estate). Yet our economy has experienced financial meltdowns that taught us that even the "safe haven" of investing in our homes isn't immune from the dangers of debt. Millions have seen the value of their homes quickly and without warning fall below the balance due on their mortgages.

Are you thinking that avoiding debt may be a good idea for most consumer items, but surely I can't expect you to pay cash for a car? Are you saying, "That would be impossible!" Yes, it is possible!

The key is to drive your current car a few more years after you finish paying for it…continuing to make the payments but into a car savings account. This creates a car fund that will enable you to pay cash for the next vehicle. In essence, you're reversing the payment cycle.

In summary, if you can't pay cash for a consumer item, don't buy it. Wait. Save. Pay cash.

Annie helped Greg reorder his thinking relative to consumer debt. He learned that making payments is not the same as being able to afford an item. Annie was wise to not just care about cash flow. She understood the wisdom that borrowers become slaves to lenders. As a result, they built their marriage on a solid financial foundation. Thanks to Annie's wisdom and Greg's willingness to learn, they showed financial maturity by forgoing current desires for future rewards and benefits.

❧ THINKING IT THROUGH ❧

❏ What is "consumer debt"?

❏ What is considered "productive debt"?

❏ Why can paying cash seem so difficult?

❏ What steps can you take to end your monthly payment cycle?

❏ Is it possible to make your monthly payments and yet have a declining net worth?

4

THE NEIGHBORS

Greg stood silently in the kitchen doorway, his unaware bride singing cheerfully. Annie's carefree serenading was a frequent reminder of how God had truly invaded his life with joy. Greg didn't want the moment to end, but with guests coming, he knew it was time to put an end to the show. Calling upon his best Rocky Balboa imitation, Greg cupped his hands and yelled, "Adrian!"

Annie turned and swung the dishtowel at Greg. "Don't do that!" she squealed. "Do you have any idea how much you scared me?"

"Not like I could have!" Greg stated, moving toward her for a makeup hug.

Backing away and catching her breath, Annie pointed at her prankster husband. "You'll pay for that, you know!"

"I'm sure I will," Greg conceded. "Now, what time would you like to serve dinner?"

Turning down the music, Annie flashed a forgiving smile. "You're the grill master. Tell me the ETA of those amazing steaks, and I'll have the sides ready on cue. I'm doing corn on the cob and twice-baked potatoes. How does that sound?"

"Nice. I'll grill at six."

"Perfect," Annie said. "I've been so looking forward to Sally and Nick coming over again. I bet it's been five or six months since we've spent time with them."

"Try eight," Greg corrected. "We haven't been with them since the Labor Day picnic. It's kind of weird. We hardly ever see them, and they live right next door. We tried a couple of times, but they canceled, remember?"

"Yes," Annie agreed. "They're busy but they're also gone a lot. When Nick travels, Sally goes to her mom's. On the weekends they usually go up and work on their new lake cabin. That's why we hardly see them at church. Who knows, maybe they'll invite us up there sometime! Anyway, they're coming tonight, so let's really enjoy our time together."

"I'll try my best," Greg mumbled as he turned to walk out.

"What was that?" Annie questioned.

"I said, I'll try my best," Greg repeated, turning to see his wife's response.

"What do you mean, Greg? Since when do you have to try with Nick and Sally?" Annie asked. "We're talking about a couple we've done everything with. We rode to church together when we co-taught the new members class. Have you forgotten how close we've been? They are some of the best friends we've had since moving here."

"'Had' is the key word," Greg said. "Things are different now. It's not just that they're gone a lot. They're not really here when they are here. Have you noticed that?"

"I see they're busy, but obviously you see something else," Annie said.

"Look, honey, I don't want to make a big deal about this. I'm not judging them…let's just say I'm really concerned. Okay?"

"Concerned about what?" Annie persisted. "Their marriage?

Nick's job? What do you mean? You just said we haven't seen them in eight months. Why are you concerned all of a sudden?"

"It's really not all of a sudden, Annie. I've sensed distance from Nick for over a year. When we were doing that financial study at church, Nick and I met during the week to go over the material. We talked about everything, but as soon as the study was finished we quit meeting. First, their travel schedule took them out of the group. Then he merged with the firm downtown, which created a long commute and a whole new circle of friends for him. Now they're always buying something or going somewhere. They never sit still. Honestly, Nick reminds me of me before you came along and straightened me out."

Annie smiled.

"I know this game, Annie. When Nick started to travel, I gave him CDs from church to try to keep him in the loop, but he never commented on any of them. One day I asked him what he thought about the sermon series at church. He said he hadn't had the time to listen to them. It's like he's turned off to spiritual things. The few times we've gotten together, all he talked about was work. Nick's different. And, frankly, I don't enjoy being around him that much."

Annie didn't say a word. She merely looked at Greg and waited for more.

"You know, I wanted to tell you this earlier, but I thought you'd probably get mad at me so I decided to keep it to myself."

"Mad at you? Why would I get mad at you? And why did you choose to keep 'it' to yourself? Now you're starting to scare me, Greg," Annie said with concern.

Greg took a seat at the kitchen counter. He knew he was in too deep to stop now. "Remember the big snowstorm right after Christmas?"

"How could I forget? I was stranded at my sister's!"

"Yeah, right. Well, the Jacksons were stranded at the cabin, so Sally called to see if we could go over and make sure their cat had water and food and to pick up the mail. You know, just check on things. I told her you were gone, but I'd be glad to do that. For the next four days I went over and checked on their house and cat."

"And the point?" Annie questioned.

"Well, when I gathered their mail during those four days, I couldn't help but notice something," Greg said.

"What do you mean you 'noticed something'?" Annie asked. "Greg, please don't tell me you read our neighbors' mail!"

"No, I didn't read their mail! But this is why I didn't mention something earlier. I knew you'd say that! Look, for the first two days I never gave their mail a second thought. That's the truth. But on the third day, I dropped the bundle of mail in the snow. I didn't want to put wet mail on the stack, so once inside I grabbed some paper towels, laid the mail out, wiped it down, and left it to dry. And that's when I noticed there were two credit card statements. And the next day, when I put the mail on the stack, I noticed three others. Annie, they received five credit card and two department store statements in four days! And that's not all. Remember when my payroll deposit got messed up, and we got those pink-slip over-drafts from First Bank? A few of those were in their mail too."

"So you did read their mail, didn't you, Greg?" Annie accused.

"Don't miss the point. I'm trying to say something here," Greg pleaded. "I'm trying to tell you I'm really concerned that our good friends next door may be in financial trouble."

"But you don't know that," Annie persisted. "Give them the benefit of the doubt. Nick's a good businessman. They're both strong Christians. And it's obvious God is blessing the new business. They belong to the club now, just bought that lake cabin, and Sally just got a Land Rover. They also sat right there in our den and reviewed financial principles with us when the church did that Bible study on money. Nick and Sally know better than to get caught up in money trouble. Promise me you won't mess up tonight by bringing up wild speculation, Greg."

𝕄

The Lie: "The trappings of wealth are a good indicator of one's financial condition."

At first glance it's easy to get caught up in the twists of this story. Did Greg jump to conclusions? Is he gossiping? Was Annie correct? Did Greg "read the Jackson's mail"? These issues could make a good debate, but to go there first would miss the core issue. The nice house, new car, lake cabin, and club membership may be a house of cards. People can look rich on the outside but be dying on the inside.

In the landmark book *The Millionaire Next Door*, Thomas Stanley wrote:

> A VP of a Trust Department made the following comments after a group focus interview with ten first-generation millionaires. "These people cannot be millionaires. They don't look like millionaires, they don't dress like millionaires, they don't eat like millionaires; they don't act like millionaires—they don't even have millionaire names. Where are the millionaires who look like millionaires?"[1]

In the comprehensive research done for their book (more than 1000 people surveyed), Thomas Stanley and William Danko found that most people think millionaires own expensive clothes, watches, and other status artifacts. In fact, that's not the case. It's more likely than not that those who appear to be financially well off *aren't*, and those who don't really look like it *are*. In most cases, those who "look like millionaires" have spent their money consuming and, therefore, don't have any real wealth. This is why the lie about the trappings of wealth is so devastating. If we look at others and then try to keep up with them, many times what we're chasing is a mirage.

Greg's perceptions of Nick and Sally's lives and lifestyle were accurate. Nick looked rich and successful, but in truth he wasn't. This could have been the same for Greg! When he met Annie, he was on the same path of destruction. He was fortunate Annie refused to go with him. Every lifestyle has a price tag. If we don't have the money today to support the life we're living, we get it another way—and that way is typically through acquiring debt. Borrowing allows us to live above our means for a season, but like a velvet noose, it's all the while closing in on us.

When God uses words like "slavery" and "bondage," He's not being dramatic; He's simply being accurate. He didn't give us the Bible to make us smarter sinners. He gave us the Bible to renew our minds and transform our lives! The last thing believers need to do is live just like the people in the world do. So why do we try? Because we become dependent on the very things that can destroy us.

> **THE TRUTH: "Therefore this is what the Holy One of Israel says: 'Because you have rejected this message, *relied* on oppression and depended on deceit, this sin will become for you like a high wall, cracked and bulging, that collapses suddenly, in an instant'" (Isaiah 30:12-13 NIV).**

Isaiah 30:1-12 has a lot to say about a child of God who lives in rebellion. Isaiah tells us this person doesn't act like a child of God, no longer listens to God's instruction, and prefers illusion to truth.

We can easily see how the "high wall" can pertain to debt. Nick and Sally had chosen to live by financial lies instead of heeding the message of God's Word.

Isaiah goes even deeper. He hits us with a shocker that is pointed at those who don't follow God's instructions. Not only can a child of God be oppressed, but he can come to *rely on oppression and depend on deceit*. How can that be? Why would a believer rely on oppression?

Simple. It makes him feel safe.

Any attachment promising fulfillment
other than God is a fraud.

The word "relied" in verse 12 is based on the Hebrew word *batach*. It means "to attach oneself, to trust, confide in, feel safe." The Hebrew word for "oppression" indicates domination "by means of fraud or extortion...a thing deceitfully gotten." When we borrow to sustain our lifestyle, there is a brief sense of feeling safe. We feel like we have something we need, something we can trust in. The problem is that *perceived safety* is a fraud. It's a "slave master in waiting."

We were created with a nature that desires to attach and depend so we will want to migrate to God, to attach and depend and find safety in Him. To entice us, Satan offers alternate attachments masquerading as fulfillments of our needs. But any attachment promising fulfillment other than God is a fraud. The wrong attachment means a growing dependency on something other than God. I've observed that excessive consumer debt is a good barometer that people are more attached to the world than they are to God. They refuse to depend on or wait on God to provide their needs, so credit cards become their answer.

No one really knows everything about their friends, which is probably for the best. And we don't really need to know everything about the people next door, in our church, or in our small groups. But we can learn from people who are making financial mistakes. We need to be conscious of the traps that can potentially destroy us. Could this be what happened to Nick and Sally? Did they sever their attachment to God and His principles? Did they forsake the biblical financial principles they'd learned and move away from their relationships with their church and friends to chase success the way the world defines it? If so, how did they get caught in that trap?

We know they didn't set out to be oppressed and depend on deceit. No couple gets married and chooses financial bondage as a goal. I think the "frog in the boiling water" story is the best analogy here. If you put a frog in a pan of hot water it will immediately jump out to save its life. However, if you put a frog in a pan of cool water and slowly turn up the heat, the change is so gradual the frog won't realize the danger until it's too late to save itself.

This highlights an important principle regarding finances. When many couples get married and have good cash flow, too often they don't take the time to make sure they're spending less than they earn. After all, a little debt with a few small monthly payments is no big deal. But let's look at what can happen.

A married couple with a combined income of $80,000 could easily spend twice that amount in a year. How is that possible? First, our couple spends $45,000 for basic living expenses, $15,000 for taxes, $5,000 for retirement contributions, and tithe $8,000. This totals $73,000, with an annual margin of $7000. Next, they buy a new car on a $50,000 note. In addition, they set up a new media room, which costs $8000, furnish their new house using a no-interest, buy now/pay later plan that takes another $10,000. And then there's the ski trip and vacation to Europe ("We need to do it before the kids come along") that took $9000 and was financed on credit cards. These big expenses aren't paid from their salaries, but are financed with interest through auto notes, store credit, and credit cards. Yes, they can "cash flow" the monthly payments on these debts from their $80,000 income, but in reality they've spent $73,000 on annual expenses and borrowed $77,000 ($50,000 + $8000 + $10,000 + $9000)!

> It is three times as hard to get
> out of debt as it is to get into debt.

Let's look at another example. Instead of Greg and Annie spending $40,000 to live on, let's say they spend $41,000 annually. That doesn't seem too bad, right? They're only overspending by $83 a month or $1000 a year. But if they do this for 10 years they'll have $10,000 in consumer debt! (This is less than the estimated average of $14,250 per household in credit card debt for Americans in 2011!)

Now, let's assume Greg and Annie's debt averages 10 percent interest, just to keep the math simple. The annual interest cost would be $1000. So here's the big question: How much does this couple need to reduce their current lifestyle to pay back that debt and keep current with the interest?

Did you figure it out?

I have spoken to hundreds of groups over the years and posed this exact situation. Do you know the most common answer I get? People usually say $2000 (the $1000 of principal plus $1000 of interest). Sometimes I hear $2100. (I have no idea where they come up with that). I rarely hear the correct answer of $3000! Most everyone sees the need to pay the principal ($1000) and the interest ($1000) so they arrive at the $2000 answer. The piece almost everyone misses is that our couple needs to *quit overspending* the $1000 that got them into this mess in the first place. Their debt is three times harder to get out of as it was to get into. Living expenses have to be cut by $3000 to start the debt repayment. This is why a healthy fear of debt is a good thing!

Annie's ultimatum to Greg about debt kept them from this future bondage. Too bad Nick and Sally didn't follow the same path. Is it really worth it to overspend $1000 a year when we know we'll have to *under spend* by $3000 someday? This financial version of Psalm 23, which one of my firm's partners wrote, puts debt in perspective:

> *The Visa card is my shepherd, I shall not want.*
> *It maketh me to lie down in debt-laden comfort,*
> *It leadeth me into malls,*
> *It restoreth my soul,*
> *It leadeth me along the paths of fellow debtors,*
> *For it has my name embossed on it.*
> *Yea, though I walk through the valley of the shadow of*
> *   bankruptcy, I will fear no balance,*
> *For Thy credit limit and minimum payments they*
> *   comfort me.*
> *Thou preparest a table before me in the presence of*
> *   my creditors.*
> *Thou anointest my balance sheet with debt.*
> *My expiration date, it runneth out.*
> *Yea, surely minimum payments will follow me the rest*
> *   of my life,*
> *And I will dwell in the house of financial bondage forever.*

I believe few people really weigh the true price of the toys and luxuries they go into debt to purchase:

- *Emotional price.* There is an incredible amount of

emotional energy spent on finances as people constantly worry about how they're going to make the next payment, what happens if their income goes down, what they'll do if they don't get the next deal. Rather than having the necessary emotional energy to focus on their marriage relationship or their children, they spend their time constantly thinking about money and feeling the burden of their debt load.

- *Economic price.* Debt always has the first priority on people's funds. The lender gets paid before anyone else. Before they can pay utilities, buy clothes, or even buy basics like groceries, they must pay the lender. If the debt load becomes so great that it outstrips all other uses, people are often forced into bankruptcy. I've had clients whose outflow exceeded their inflow to the point they couldn't even buy the necessities. This lack of economic freedom leads to oppressive bondage, which is a tough price to pay.

- *Spiritual price.* Debt payments have a higher call on people's income than giving and being generous. Is it any wonder that Christians don't look any different than people of the world when it comes to giving? As someone once said, "If Christ were to return and take back all the Christians who didn't have debt, the rapture may have already occurred." Why? Because Christians, for the most part, don't look any different or live any differently than people in the world.

The spiritual price that debt extracts is even greater when we consider that people are storing up treasures in heaven with their giving. In Matthew 5, we read that we're to store up treasures in heaven where moth and rust do not destroy and thieves do not break in and steal. People need to realize their giving is inextricably linked to their eternal rewards. In 1 Timothy 6:17-19, we find out that we lay a solid foundation by being generous. So anytime Christians neglect giving (and debt impinges on that), we are laying a shaky foundation and will have less in the future and in heaven.

> We can't leave a positive legacy on the home front if we are never home.

- *Family price.* Many times, debt makes developing an intentional plan for our children hard to implement because there's no time or freedom to focus on it. People have to create their next source of income, make the next deal, or work overtime to fund their debt payments. Financial stress puts undue strain on marriages, accelerates the pace of life, and reduces time with family. And parents cannot build character into their children in a hurry. We can't leave a positive legacy on the home front if we are never home.

I don't regret staying out of consumer debt because it reduced financial pressure and allowed me more time with my family. It allowed time for intentional focus on building a positive legacy (see chapter 13 for more on legacy).

Isn't it time to obey the truth of God's Word regarding debt and experience the resulting freedom? I encourage you, no matter where you are currently with debt, to start moving in the direction of living debt free. Start paying off your consumer debt and credit card debt, and then move on to paying off your car and then your house. Julie and I have never regretted the decision we made decades ago to follow this path.

One more observation about God's Word and His principles. Although they can be difficult to implement and sometimes don't seem to make sense today, God's principles are always true and always right. His children never regret implementing them. So why not make a decision today to live for God like Greg and Annie did? Even though they may not look prosperous to outsiders, Greg and Annie probably have a better chance of becoming the "millionaire next door" than Nick and Sally.

ৠ THINKING IT THROUGH ৡ

❑ Which couple do you identify with most: Greg and Annie or Nick and Sally? Explain.

❑ Remember the principle of *batach*? Have you attached or come to rely on debt to meet your needs?

❑ Have you purchased things with money you don't have to impress people?

❑ Explain the "three times as easy to get into debt as it is to get out" principle in your own words.

❑ What steps will you take to move toward debt-free living?

5

THE DINNER MEETING

"Well, Greg?" Annie pleaded. "Will you? Will you promise not to bring up your concern about Nick and Sally's finances tonight? They are our friends, and they're coming over for a relaxing dinner—not a financial audit."

Seeing Annie's concern, Greg took her hand and carefully chose his words. "You know, Annie, when we first met, I thought I had a lot of things about life all together. I didn't. I was very immature, especially when it came to handling money. I didn't know what money was, where it came from, or what to do with it. What's worse, I had no fear of debt. I was totally deceived. But you saw that deception right away, and you spoke truth into my life about it. Remember?"

"Of course," Annie replied. "I'm surprised you put up with me during those budgeting sessions. I did come on a little strong."

"That's an understatement," Greg said with a smile. "But how strong you came on isn't the point. The key is *what* you said to me. You cared enough to tell me the truth. In fact, you were willing to risk our relationship for what you believed. And that willingness to take a risk changed my life. Now I want to ask you something, okay?"

Annie nodded.

"Did you ever go into our budgeting sessions planning to wreck the evening?"

"Of course not," Annie replied quickly. "Why would you even ask that?"

"Well, if you remember, those sessions got pretty heated. Are you sure you didn't come over planning to change my attitude and set me straight?"

"Greg, you know better than that!" Annie responded in surprise. "I went into those sessions prayerfully wanting the best for us. I shared what I believed God expected from two people about to be married. That's all I ever tried to do. God did the rest. You know that."

Greg smiled and waited for Annie's words to sink in. And when she smiled back, he squeezed her hand. "Yes, I do know that," he said. "Now, what do you say we just go into tonight prayerfully wanting the best for our friends?"

"I think that would be a great idea. Let's do just that," Annie replied.

Greg and Annie set about getting ready for company and preparing for the barbecue. When the Jacksons arrived, dinner went off without a hitch. Conversation flowed effortlessly between the two couples. The time passed quickly, and it felt like the four of them had never been apart. Everyone agreed that spending time together was long overdue.

As the evening began to wind down, the two women were enjoying their last bites of cheesecake when Nick clinked his coffee cup to get everyone's attention.

"Is this going to be an espresso toast?" Greg joked.

Nick chuckled along with the others, but it was obvious he had something he wanted to say. As he paused, Sally slid closer and took his hand.

"Actually, this is more of an announcement than a toast," Nick said, looking at his wife.

Sally smiled and nodded.

"Well, first of all I want you guys to know how great it is for Sally and me to be here tonight," Nick said. "It means a lot to us. It really does. But this is more than just a visit. Sally and I really needed this."

"Oh, that's sweet, Nick," Annie said. "But all we did was grill some steaks, play Catch Phrase, and hang out. We didn't do anything special."

"But that's just it," Nick said. "You didn't have to do or say anything special. You guys are doing what you always do. You are here for us. You are being real!" Nick looked at Sally and then at Greg and Annie before continuing. "Look, let me put it this way. I feel like there's an elephant in the room. He's sitting right there on the coffee table blocking my view. I need to acknowledge that big gray guy is here so I can see through him. Frankly, I'm tired. No, Sally and I are tired of carrying that guy everywhere we go. We need your help."

Nick paused for a moment and buried his face in his hands. Looking up he said, "I don't even know where to start. The best way to describe the past two years is just to say we've been very caught up in…in getting ahead, I guess."

Greg and Annie exchanged glances.

"We feel like we haven't been honest with you…with our friends. It might have started when I merged my company with…No, by then it had already started. The real problem is that little by little Sally and I started compromising on what we knew to be true—on the principles we learned in that Bible study on finances we did together.

"I got busy. I shot for the gold. And I mixed in with people who could make things happen *only because* they could make things happen. We traded wise counsel for unwise counsel. As a result, we took on debt to buy a lot of things we thought we needed to 'look the part' with the new business and our new friends. But we weren't satisfied or happy. To assuage the emptiness that crept into our lives and marriage, we bought more stuff to fill in the gaps. That brought more debt. The bottom line is that we got caught up in lies about money…that it could bring us happiness and contentment and peace of mind. It's as simple as that—and as painful as that."

Everyone sat quietly for a moment. Greg broke the silence. "Hey, Nick and Sally, it's okay. We're here for you two. You can tell us anything. You know that. There's no condemnation here. Never was. Never will be."

Annie nodded in agreement.

"Since 'the elephant' is out on the table," Greg continued, "would it be all right if I ask something personal?"

"Sure," Nick replied. "Ask away."

"When you first saw that things were getting out of hand, did you think about talking to us? I mean we've talked about everything. Why didn't you call or share with us what was going on? Don't you think we would have been here for you?"

"That's a great question, Greg. And you don't know how many times we wanted to do that," Nick answered. "In fact, Sally and I talked about calling you two several times. We knew we were straying. We saw that a year ago. And even though we knew you both knew how we thought about money at the end of the day, we always came to the same conclusion."

"What was that?" Greg asked.

"What we choose to do with our money is our business," Nick responded. "And that stopped us."

THE LIE: "What we do with our money is
our business."

Nick and Sally aren't alone in buying into this money lie. For some reason, our money—more than almost any other issue in our lives—is not to be discussed with other people. It's taboo. We talk about personal relationship issues, health issues, spiritual issues, addictions to pornography and drugs, but we don't talk about money.

We'll look at why this is the case a bit later, but the fact is we cannot hide our financial lives. The One who really matters already knows.

> **THE TRUTH:** "Nothing in all creation is hidden from God's sight. Everything is uncovered and laid bare before the eyes of him to whom we must give account" (Hebrews 4:13 NIV).

This verse and others like it take us to a place we rarely go on our own. It brings us face-to-face with two very sobering truths. First, everything we do is done before God. Second, you and I will give an account for everything we do when we face Him on the last day.

I know it's hard for some people to swallow, but there are some issues in life we need help with. I've found over the years that money is one area where we all need accountability. Why? Because when it comes to money, we can convince ourselves of almost anything we want to believe. "I deserve the bigger house!" "That is the perfect grill for me!" "Yes, we really do need that outdoor fireplace!"

When it comes to our relationship with that wad in our pocket or that pile in the bank, we aren't short on biblical truth. God built in financial accountability with the people of Israel. It is called *the tithe*. Think about it. The commitment of tithing guides us into being good managers of our finances.

It's estimated that the average Christian gives less than 2.4 percent of his or her income to charity. Not tithing implies that we can't or aren't living within our means and that we're not accountable to God's principles. Poor money management also seems to be a doorway into other problems. Have you ever wondered what financial condition the U.S. might be in right now if our country had the accountability of a balanced budget?

> Knowledge may be the doorway to
> change, but we need to walk through it.

Accountability can come in many forms. For the do-it-yourselfer, there are multiple financial courses, books, and seminar training to choose from. Some people seem capable of reforming their bad habits. They can turn their lives around. If this is you, I encourage you to clean up your financial act. If you don't have money for these advice resources, you can get biblically sound financial information from Dave Ramsey and other Christians by clicking on the radio, going online, and checking out their books from the library.[1]

The truth is that a lot of us won't be successful in reforming our finances on our own. Just like many dieters need Weight Watchers or other programs for accountability, most individuals need some type of financial support network to make a long-term change in their finances.

Most of us agree that our biblical knowledge is far greater than our desire to obey what we know. Nick and Sally had been through a financial Bible study. They knew the truth; they just weren't applying it. For many people, financial accountability based on biblical truth can make the difference between success and failure. Plugging into a small group, finding a mentor, or starting a financial study with other people may be very useful.[2]

For more than three decades, Ronald Blue & Co. has operated on the simple value proposition of encouraging and holding people accountable to applying the biblical principles of money to achieve peace of mind. We've found that whether folks are overspenders like Nick and Sally or have more than enough, many need to hire financial advisors to provide the accountability and solutions to get them on a better financial path. If it applies, we urge you to seek this type of one-on-one help.

Nick and Sally are far from fiction. They represent all of us who know what to do and choose not to do it. Knowledge may be the doorway to change, but we need to walk through it.

Money is an emotionally charged subject. We earn it. We deposit it. And, as Christians, we know we are supposed to be good stewards of it. And we usually feel we are supposed to know how to handle it without outside help. We're often willing to get help to develop an exercise routine by seeking a trainer, start a diet by consulting a nutritionist, and overcome an addiction by talking with a counselor. Why is it so difficult to seek help in the financial arena? I believe there are several reasons:

- *Pride.* Since money is viewed as a measure of our success and worth, we're afraid to let anyone else in on our position. Once we open our financial window, we can no longer put on a façade or create the illusion we're better off than we really are. It's humbling to open our checkbooks to someone else's scrutiny.

- *Embarrassment.* We're deathly afraid of letting anyone see the true results of the financial decisions we've made. I cannot tell you how many times clients have come into our offices and their first words are, "I'm sure you have never seen or had anyone with this situation…" I always smile because there really isn't anything new under the sun. Sure the numbers and the specifics may be different, but the situations, the principles, and the solutions are the same. We all make financial mistakes. Rest assured many others have done similar things…and sometimes worse.

- *Family background.* "Wrapped up in every family history—threaded invisibly throughout the memories—is money. That's right, money. How a family gets, grapples with, guards, and gives money is all a part of who that family is. Money, in part, defines a family."[3] And yet for some reason we pass on from one generation to the next the idea that money is not to be talked about. Families are very reticent to talk about money issues. Very few dads discuss money with their children. This silence communicates a feeling that the next generation should know intuitively what to do with money and, as a result, doesn't need to seek accountability.

- *Pain.* Anytime people make themselves accountable, they're saying they want to change. They want to do something differently, and in many cases that difference causes pain. We may be advised we need to be on a budget to ensure we're spending less than we make. We may need to sell some of our favorite toys or possessions. We may need to downsize our homes. These types of actions are painful and, as a result, hinder our desire to seek accountability.

Nick and Sally drifted away from accountability. Their church attendance slipped, which is never a good sign. They knew they needed help, but instead of moving toward those who could help them they distanced themselves. They tried to cover up their situation by getting further from truth and substituting things, and the subsequent debt, as they searched for satisfaction. How different the last few years could have been had they chosen to have even one accountability conversation.

> Two are better than one because they have a good return for their labor. For if either of them falls, the one will lift up his companion. But woe to the one who falls when there is not another to lift him up. Furthermore, if two lie down together they keep warm, but how can one be warm alone? And if one can overpower him who is alone, two can resist him. A cord of three strands is not quickly torn apart (Ecclesiastes 4:9-12).

The reason we need accountability in the financial arena is because we need help to see what we cannot see ourselves. If we're going to stand before God and account for our financial decisions, shouldn't we get started on the accountability part now? Accountability is big in our Christian world. And it is one of the reasons many churches have small groups and why mentors are so good to have. We don't need people to write our checks or balance our checkbooks, but we do need them to check our motives and offer biblically sound advice. A final accounting is coming, so let's start preparing now.

◊ Thinking It Through ◊

❏ Is there any area in your life you wish you could change?

❏ How successful have you been in changing that area on your own?

❏ What person can you talk to or group can you join to increase your chance of success?

❏ Do you know a couple or individual who might benefit if you (and your spouse, if you're married) spent more time with them or mentored them?

❏ Does your church have a financial Bible study or course you can particpate in? If not, are you interested in starting one? If so, check out www.crown.org or www.daveramsey.com for suggestions and resources.

❏ Why do you think accountability in the money area is so difficult?

6

THE TIPPING POINT

In his bestseller *The Tipping Point: How Little Things Make a Big Difference,* Malcolm Gladwell describes social events in which a previously rare phenomenon becomes dramatically more common in a group or culture. Gladwell defines a "tipping point" as "the moment of critical mass, the threshold, the boiling point." His book is a great read, filled with case studies that validate his tagline. The little things can indeed make a big difference.

In a very real sense, budgets are tipping points. Our numbers form a critical mass, placing us on the threshold of clarity. But financial clarity is a rare phenomenon. Most Americans don't really know where they are financially. That's part of the reason budgets become boiling points for so many. We don't always like what we find out. Clarity has a way of tipping us over, but it can also set us free.

Let me come clean here. When it came to writing this chapter, I (Kelly Talamo) didn't have to dig for content or fish for illustrations. Everything I needed was in the mirror. This chapter (as well as others) doesn't *just* hit close to home, this *is* my home. In fact, if there's one specific lie that's really tripped me up, the lie covered in this chapter is it. So let me be clear. I'm not here to give you excellent advice on budgeting (I'll let Russ do that). I'm here to expose a lie that can keep you from budgeting for financial freedom. Let me put it another way: "No budget = no freedom."

Here's what I do know about budgeting. It matters! It matters if we budget and if we don't. It matters in the present; it matters for the future. And, just in case you're anything like me, perhaps you believe budgeting may not matter that much in *your* life. In fact, maybe you couldn't care less about budgeting. But it does matter to your long-term well-being. And if you're married and have children, it matters to your spouse and family. That's one lesson I learned the hard way.

I'm an entrepreneur. I start things. I'm artistic and creative. Consequently, I never sit around and think, "We really need more structure around here." My wife, Mary, is the polar opposite. She loves structure. She wanted to start budgeting together when we got engaged. She was talking about saving for our daughters' weddings before we even had them! And whenever she mentioned the "B" word, I could almost feel my throat tighten as I felt like I was gasping for air. I'd think, "Where did this woman come from?" I almost (not quite) saw it as a good excuse not to marry her.

Whether it was selling cars, designing landscapes, or giving speeches, God has always allowed me to make money for our family. *Making* it has never been my problem. But *directing* money to the proper place has been a different story altogether.

Early in our marriage, no matter how much money I made, there was never any left at the end of the year. If I made $30,000, then $30,000 made ends meet. If I made $52,000 the next year, then $52,000 made ends meet. I consistently made a little more annually, but the increase had little effect on my financial scenario. I was perplexed. It's one thing to have a bad year and end up with no money. I understand that concept. But to continually break even when every year my income got better and better? That was a puzzle I couldn't solve. Was it the new tractor I bought or the home improvements we made? Was it the private school tuition or medical bills? Was it simply the fact we now had three kids? All contributing factors I'm sure, but I knew in my heart there was more to the story. Either something was wrong or something was missing. And either way, I had to find out because as much as I enjoyed working all year long, I rarely found myself looking forward to Christmas because of the financial stress. That was sad for me and frustrating for Mary.

Mary and I have always had a strong marriage anchored in good communication. But whenever the subject of finances came up, it wasn't hard to sense her frustration. As strong as we were as a couple, talking about money would always tip us over. Then one day Mary approached me with something ridiculous. "You know, we really need to start saving some money."

When she said that, I let her have it. "Hey, God gives us all we need. I'm doing all I can. If you think we need more, then you go out and get it."

Sensing I wasn't having one of my more spiritual moments, Mary put it back on me. "Kelly, you really need to get some help because whatever this issue is, it's way bigger than you!"

It's very easy for Christians to spiritualize shortcomings. And concerning this area of budgeting, I did it with gusto. I knew that I was coming up short, but instead of digging deeper to find out why, I rationalized the problem (using Scripture, no less). I spouted that God promised to supply all our needs (Philippians 4:19). So there it was. We asked Him for our "daily bread," and the last time I looked the kids hadn't missed a meal.

Mary and I loved everything about our church, especially the small fellowship groups. That's where we discussed the practical things, including honoring our parents, raising kids, and handling money. That's also where I met Russ. And after a few short hallway conversations, Russ agreed to meet with me one-on-one.

Meeting with Russ was nothing like I thought it would be. I went in expecting a private financial seminar, yet we never opened a book, filled out a form, or looked at a spreadsheet. Instead, Russ let me talk as much as I wanted. I told him how I could easily make money but never seemed to have any left. I was honest and shared my frustrations with this constant break-even scenario and how it was beginning to weigh on Mary.

Russ listened intently. He was gracious. He told me, "You know, this really isn't rocket science. In fact it's pretty simple." Then he took a piece of paper and drew little boxes to illustrate the five places that money could go. I didn't want to look dumb, so I nodded my head like I understood everything. Then Russ repeated the information just to make sure I got it.

Around our third session in, when we were about to wrap up, Russ hit me with something I never saw coming. He calmly said, "Hey, the next time you come over, bring your business checkbook with you." At first I was stunned. In fact, my first thought was, "Okay, here's where the financial planner takes over my money." So I tried to play it really cool. "Ah, my checkbook! Hey, Russ, you know all of this is new to me. I'm happy to tell you how much I have and how much I make. But why do you need my checkbook? I didn't know you wanted to spend my money for me."

Russ didn't flinch. He simply smiled and said, "I don't want to spend your money. I just need to see where it goes."

"Where it goes? What do you mean?"

"Well," he replied, "money is just a tool, but it's a tool we need to take charge of. All your money is going somewhere. If you don't know where it's going, you'll never be able to use it wisely. Next time you come, bring your checkbook."

Wow. The guy was dead serious.

The next time, I brought the man my checkbook. I didn't like it, but I did it. And I can still see that moment when I handed it over. I knew this was so right! I remember thinking, "My life will never be the same." I was finally getting help for something bigger than me.

The operation was quick and painless. Russ walked through my checkbook page after page, stopping along the way to ask me questions about a few purchases. I answered him honestly, and he moved on to the next item. I never felt grilled or the least bit condemned. Instead, I felt more and more free.

When the survey ended, Russ was quite candid. "I see where your money goes, and except for the fact you're a little impulsive, it's pretty good. Your problem isn't what you spend money on. Your problem is what you *don't*. You don't have money put aside for capital expenditures or an emergency fund. And I don't think you're putting enough money aside for taxes, and this oversight probably bites you at the end of the year. Those are the things you need to include in your budget."

I was listening.

Russ continued. "Bottom line, you're not breaking even at all. You're falling behind. So you really need two budgets—one for your home and one for your business."

There it was again, the dreaded "B" word...only this time in stereo!

Russ never taught me how to budget. He didn't have to. Remember, it's not rocket science. In fact, the mechanics of budgeting are easy. Most budgets fit on one sheet of paper. How hard can that be for two educated people?

So what throws people for a loop? Everything else. It takes time to budget. Two people have to come together and agree on things. Both have to show up and be willing to be honest. We have to get "in the light" and stay in the light. And speaking truth in the light may be the hardest thing of all.

Needless to say, my mindset on finances didn't change overnight. Mary had totally adjusted to how I was wired and always respected the way God made me, so it took me a long time to see things her way. In fact, I didn't even want to try until I met with Russ.

A few months later, Russ asked me how I was coming with my budget. Up until then he hadn't pressed me for anything specific. He'd just occasionally reinforce how important it was to create one. This particular day I was a little touchy, and our exchange went something like this: "Look, Russ, you know it's not that easy for me. I'm doing everything you said, separating business and personal. I'm working on it. But it's impossible to budget when I don't even know how much money I'll make. You know my income is up and down!" (I thought I had him on that one.)

Russ wasn't fazed. "Yes, but you know how much you need, right? Start with your needs and work back from there. Don't tell me you 'can't' budget. Anyone can budget. Just start with what you know you've got to have."

That was so clear even I could see it. Sensing he might not stop there, I decided to get a little more transparent. "Okay, I get that. But I just have to tell you that I hate this kind of stuff. I really do. To sit down and look at what we spent on car insurance last month or what the light bill is going to be three months from now... really? That doesn't do a thing for me. In fact, I'm fine without it!"

"Well, you might be fine without it, but I can tell you Mary is not," Russ shot back.

I didn't say a word.

Thankfully, Russ started talking again. "Look, Kelly. I know you're making money, giving, paying your taxes, and all of that. I see it. But if you want real peace in your home, you need to do this for Mary. That's how God wired her, and she deserves your cooperation."

Bang! That was it. That's when I started to see just how much a budget matters.

We are never freer than when
we have a budget and stick to it.

Mary and I didn't change overnight. In fact, budgeting is still the easiest thing for me (not us) to abandon. But here are some cold facts about our finances. When we budget, we spend less than we make. When we don't, we spend more than we make. When we budget, we know where we stand. When we don't, we only assume we do. And every time I've assumed anything about our finances, I'm dead wrong. *Every single time.*

I said earlier that a budget itself isn't difficult. Budgets merely expose any problem areas we already have. If we overspend on entertainment or simply have way too much house, the numbers will expose it. If our car payments are double what we give back to God, the numbers will expose that too. And if we live way below what we can really afford, the numbers will affirm us in that too. We may lie, but numbers don't. That's what's really hard about a budget. It puts what we say is important in its "real" category. We are "in the light."

When it came to budgeting, I bought into a huge lie. Maybe it's the biggest lie of all!

The Lie: "Budgets are too restrictive."

I said this over and over and over. I said it so much I believed it was true. It's not. There's nothing restrictive about budgets. In fact, we are never freer than when we have a budget and stick to it. Never!

> **THE TRUTH:** "Know well the condition of your flocks, and pay attention to your herds; for riches are not forever, nor does a crown endure to all generations" (Proverbs 27:23-24).

Time for me (Russ) to chime in. I remember when I first met Kelly. He was a gifted communicator and taught several Sunday school classes I attended. When we got to the money deal, it was just as he shared. He claimed that he made enough money but could never save any. Mary and Kelly were like so many couples. They had never sat down and developed a plan to make sure they were spending less than they made.

The key to financial independence
is never how much you make
but how much you spend.

I've found that this is one of the great secrets to financial peace of mind: *If we spend less than we make, and we do it for a long time with a positive cash flow margin, we will develop a very positive financial situation.* Saving is wise. The ability to create "margin" by keeping our ongoing expenses low will serve all of us extremely well over our lifetimes. Anyone—at any income level—who has trouble setting and keeping a spending plan that incorporates their values and goals will likely have a lifelong struggle in their financial situation.

As Kelly shared earlier, there are five places our money can go: giving, taxes, living expenses, debt repayment, cash flow margin.

The Uses of Money

When I met with Kelly and Mary, I helped them fill in the "little boxes" with target amounts to ensure they were spending less than they made and knew where their money was going. I took them through these steps:

Step 1: Determine their giving amount.

Step 2: Prepare an income tax projection and set aside tax withholdings accordingly.

Step 3: Build in minimum debt repayments as part of the budget.

Once these three boxes were filled in, they needed to complete a "living expense plan" or budget. The key to success is threefold: 1) Do not leave any expense category unbudgeted; 2) Be realistic about amounts; 3) Implement a system that works for you (more on systems later). A Living Expense worksheet you can use as a guide is located in the appendix.

So why not get started? Create a "little boxes" chart and fill in the amounts. Once that is done, double check to make sure the top box (income) is enough to cover all the outflow. If it's not, you'll need to go back to the living expense sheet and make adjustments. Taxes, debt payments, and giving get the first dollars out of your paycheck, and they usually cannot be changed. Remember when we said earlier that one of the challenges with debt is that it has first call on your money? This is where it shows up.

An often overlooked principle is to make sure you have a *positive margin* each year. This means some money for savings coming out each month or at the end of each year. Author G.K. Chesterton said, "There are two ways to get enough. One is to accumulate more and the other is to desire less."

In my more than 30 years of working in the financial services industry, I can say that it's almost impossible to earn enough if you never learn to control your expenses. So regardless of your income level, living on a healthy budget will always pay dividends long term. The key to financial independence is never how much you make but how much you spend. Take control of your living expenses. And the lower those expenses are, the better.

The acid test to knowing whether you're on track with your budget (or, as my wife likes to call it, a "spending plan"—she doesn't like the "B" word) is to be able to tell at any point in time where you are against your predetermined standard. For example, say you've budgeted $2000 for vacations. It's now March 31, and you've already spent $1000. You have a trip to Hawaii planned for September that will cost $2000. You instantly know you have a problem. Budgets should tell you how much you've already spent and how much you have left to spend.

This principle runs true about utilities, eating out, auto repairs, and all the other categories. You need to know how you are doing against a standard you've set or predetermined, along with being able to say how much you've spent so far.

I've met many individuals who say they're on a budget because they can show me a nice "summary" they've done using Quicken or other financial software. These programs are useful for determining where your money is going and setting initial budget amounts, but they aren't always helpful in controlling spending. I've learned over the years that whatever budget system is used, they all end up being like an "envelope system."

What's an envelope system? First create (or imagine) envelopes for each area of your budget. After deciding how much to allocate on a spending area, you put that amount of money in the labeled envelope. You pay for that particular expense out of the envelope until the money is gone. (The "envelope" doesn't have to be a physical envelope. It can be a combination of real envelopes, checkbooks, checkbook registers, debit cards, and credit cards.) The point is that you don't spend any more than what's in an envelope on that expense until the next budget cycle.[1]

> Budgeting is telling your money
> where you want it to go rather than
> wondering where it went.

Many people I've counseled have two or three discretionary areas where they overspend. Once they learn to control these areas, their budgets work. I encourage you to determine what these areas are for you. They may be dining out, kids' clothes, gifts, and vacations. Whatever the area(s), set aside the budgeted amount every month, and when the envelope is empty, *stop spending* in that area until the next budget cycle.

As Arthur Wellington said many years ago, "Budgeting is simply the art of doing well with one dollar what any bungler can do with two."[2] And Rudyard Kipling said, "Any fool can waste; any fool can muddle; but it takes something of a man to save, and the more he saves, the more of a man does it make of him."[3]

Julie and I have been on a financial system for the past 30 years that, in essence, has taken the principles of the envelope system and applied them by using cash, credit cards, debit cards, and checks. It doesn't matter what system you use as long as you know how you're spending against your predetermined allocation amounts at any point in time. Budgeting is telling your money where you want it to go rather than wondering where it went. This was Kelly's struggle.

After you complete the questions at the end of this chapter, this might be a good time and place for you (and, if married, your spouse) to take a break. Take some time to look hard at what's really happening in your financial world. Then, in light of what you see, make the needed adjustments. If you do this, you will learn that there is indeed freedom in financial control. Budgets are not as repressive as the evil one whispers in your ear.

❧ THINKING IT THROUGH ❧

❏ Are you on a budget? Why or why not?

❏ Have you tried to control two or three expense items? Was this effort helpful?

❏ What single expense area do you overspend in the most? What's the first step to start budgeting in this area?

❏ What is your biggest challenge to living on a spending plan?

❏ Do you typically receive an income tax refund?

❏ If you filled in the five "little boxes," was this difficult? Why or why not?

7

HAVING IT ALL

"Wow, what a ride!" Scott exclaimed as his friend brought the new BMW to an abrupt stop. "Danny Pierce! I've got to tell you, you really know how to live! This Beamer is the most amazing car I've ever ridden in. No, check that. This is the best set of wheels I've ever seen! Pop the hood, brother. I need a close-up of the power plant."

Feeling somewhat embarrassed, Danny pulled the hood release latch. Before he could get out of his seat, Scott was out of the car, ready to be face-to-face with the Beamer's engine.

"Would you look at this!" Scott said admiringly. "German engineering at its best. I don't think I've ever stood this close to auto perfection. This, my friend, is a work of art!"

"Glad you like it," Danny replied.

"Like it?" Scott questioned as he examined every detail. "That's an understatement. I don't *like* it Danny, I *love* it! If this were my rod, I'd probably sleep in this baby."

"Easy, tiger," Danny replied. "At the end of the day it's just a car."

"Easy for you to say, Captain Corporate. What is this now…

your second or third Beamer? You forget that when Friday night comes for me, I step out of my work truck."

"All in good time, Scotty," Danny responded. "All in good time."

"Seriously, Danny, I meant what I said. You really do know how to live. You really seem to have it all."

"Well, that's a stretch, Scotty. Nobody has it all. You know that," Danny replied a bit defensively.

"Well, from my seat on the bus, you're pretty darn close. I mean take a look. You've got a beautiful family, an incredible home, and a super job with a six-figure income…not to mention one of the best golf swings in the city. Now you top all that off with the Ultimate Driving Machine. What else does a guy need?"

Scott's question rang in Danny's ears like a church bell at noon. *What else does a guy need,* he thought. *Really, what else* does *a guy truly need?* As Danny pondered the question, his mind shot back to a familiar scene four years earlier.

On a much smaller driveway, he and his wife had arrived home with their first child. With vivid detail Danny recalled helping Kim out of the car and carefully walking her and the baby across their narrow gravel drive. He remembered how excited he was as they made their way up the front porch steps. He even recalled what they said as they peered at their sleeping son.

"Kim, look at how precious he is!" Danny said softly. "This little guy really completes us, doesn't he?"

"Yes, he does," Kim whispered back. "We have everything we need, Danny."

This was a moment Danny revisited many times. He called it the best moment of his life more than once. But as he thought about it this time, a myriad of questions flooded his mind. *If we really had what we needed, why did we buy a bigger house? If I didn't need any more money, why did I agree to become district manager? And why did I insist that we join the club and put in a pool? More importantly, why am I standing in this driveway, staring at this car, hesitating about telling Scotty how happy and perfect my life is?*

Each question made Danny's stomach drop. As the morning sun danced brilliantly across the Beamer's hood, he realized, *This might be the emptiest feeling I've ever had in my life.*

Contentment is never linked to
an *amount* of anything.

Noticing that Danny was somewhere else, Scott spoke up. "Hey, man, what's with you? Is something wrong? You look like you've seen a ghost!"

"No, Scotty," Danny replied. "I didn't see a ghost. But right now I sure feel like I could be one! I just discovered something is wrong."

"What are you talking about?" Scott smirked. "Did you buy the wrong color or something?"

"No," Danny said sadly. "I just realized I've bought into a lie about money."

⚭

THE LIE: "The more we have, the happier we'll be."

We've all stood where Danny is. We've been on some kind of driveway without any answers to why we're not content. We may not have been staring at a car, but what we stared at isn't the point. If we're really honest, we can probably recall moments where we stopped long enough to do the math and realized that "more" and "happiness" don't equate.

Maybe you can remember when you lost your excitement over your new car after only a few months. Or what about that boat you had to have that now sits in dry dock? And the new couch you couldn't live without or the house addition you couldn't wait to show your friends? The excitement wore off; the happiness faded.

Our appetites or desires vary greatly from person to person, but deep down inside we all have an insatiable appetite…for something…for *more*. What constitutes "more" isn't really relevant. That we have this appetite is all we really need to know. That's ground zero for being content.

> **THE TRUTH: "I have learned to be content in whatever circumstances I am" (Philippians 4:11).**

Contentment doesn't come naturally to anyone. Even the apostle Paul had to learn contentment. And if a guy with his perspective had some learning to do, how can we escape the process? Let's take a look at how Paul learned to put this truth into practice:

> Not that I speak from want, for I have learned to be content in whatever circumstances I am. I know how to get along with humble means, and I also know how to live in prosperity; in any and every circumstance I have learned the secret of being filled and going hungry, both of having abundance and suffering need. I can do all things through Him who strengthens me (Philippians 4:11-13).

When things get tough or when we find we need a little extra push, many of us who know the Bible are pretty quick to quote the last line of that passage: "I can do all things through Him who strengthens me." No argument there. But we'd miss the whole point if we didn't notice *when* Paul said this. There's a reason this verse is where it is. The context is key. You see, Paul wasn't bragging about the strength God gave him when he was planting churches in Asia or when he was shipwrecked at sea. In fact, Paul wasn't linking his strength found in Jesus Christ to any of his accomplishments (though he certainly needed it during those times). Instead, Paul is telling us that if there was one place he needed the strength of Jesus Christ, it was in *making the choice to be content.* Paul did what we need to do. He looked at every one of his circumstances and made a very specific decision. Being content was something Paul *chose.*

To be content means to be satisfied. It's looking around and saying that whatever our circumstances are, we're okay. They may not be fine, but we are. And here's the kicker. Contentment is never linked to an *amount* of anything. It's not about having everything we want or what we need. In fact, prosperity can be a rabbit trail that leads us away from contentment! Paul knew that. He'd been on top of the world personally and professionally, and he'd been on the bottom. So now he wants us to know what he has learned. He wants to clue us in on his little secret. And the secret? *No matter what we have or what we lack, we need the power of Jesus Christ to make the choice to be content.* Only His power can sustain us in the restless place that every human heart goes. His power identifies and quiets that insatiable appetite in each of us.

We wouldn't think it would be this way. We usually decide we're all destined to be a little bit restless—we all need something. So we buy the lie that what we really need is just a little more…more money…more possessions…more…This is a faulty line of thinking that leads to futility:

> How much richer we've become than at any time in the past. *USA Today* compared life today to 1980 to

show how life has changed since Ronald Reagan was elected president and during the adulthood of Baby Boomers, the 77 million born from 1946 through 1964. The average annual income was $24,079 per person in 1980 in inflation-adjusted dollars, according to the Bureau of Economic Analysis. Last year, it was $40,454 per person. What's less obvious is how much better a lifestyle can be bought with the same amount of money, whether it's $25,000 or $100,000. In 1980, 2.5 gigabytes of computer power cost $214,000 and consumed a room. Today, that capacity sells for $7 in a pinky-sized flash drive at Best Buy. The wealth of the computer era and other innovations have made this generation so prosperous that it's hard to remember what life was like not long ago. A typical new house today has 2,400 square feet and fewer people in it than the typical 1,700 square-foot new home of 1980. Today, Americans fly twice as many miles as in 1980 and own more vehicles than the nation has drivers. Yet Americans don't feel as rich as they were several years ago or when they grew up.[1]

Obviously, more and bigger incomes and more for the dollar are not the keys to feeling rich. An article in *The Atlantic* entitled "Secret Fears of the Super-Rich" summed it up well:

The respondents turn out to be a generally dissatisfied lot, whose money has contributed to deep anxieties involving love, work, and family. Indeed, they are frequently dissatisfied even with their sizable fortunes. Most of them still do not consider themselves financially secure; for that, they say, they would require on average one-quarter more wealth than they currently possess. (Remember: this is a population with assets in the tens of millions of dollars and above.) One respondent, the heir to an enormous fortune, says that what matters most to him is his Christianity, and that his greatest aspiration is "to love the Lord, my family, and my friends." He also reports that he wouldn't feel financially secure until he had $1 billion in the bank.[2]

Can you believe it? It would take him one billion dollars to feel comfortable.

Only knowing and establishing a relationship with Jesus Christ can put a stop to this madness. With the mind of the indwelling Christ, we can gain insights into what we really need. We get divine perspective. Then through His power we can make the right decisions. We can decide to be something most of the world is not. *We can decide to be content.* That is one thing Jesus Christ *will always* give us the strength to do. That's the truth; that's the secret.

Money and stuff cannot bring satisfaction.

If we ignore this truth of being content in any circumstance through the strength of Christ—especially in the financial arena—we typically "spend more than we make" to try to have more to feel content about. We feel that a "little more" stuff or one more "thing" will get us to the point of contentment. So we buy it even if we don't have the money. And this typically puts us in debt and takes away the freedom we desire. Money and stuff cannot bring satisfaction.

Wayne Dyer said it well: "When I chased after money, I never had enough. When I got my life on purpose and focused on giving of myself and everything that arrived into my life, then I was prosperous."[3] He sounds a lot like Solomon, who summed up in Ecclesiastes 5:10-11: "He who loves money will not be satisfied with money, nor he who loves abundance with its income. This too is vanity. When good things increase, those who consume them increase. So what is the advantage to their owners except to look on?"

This anonymous quote puts the futility of more "things" in perspective:

> Mr. and Mrs. Thing are a very pleasant and successful couple. At least, that's the verdict of most people who tend to measure success with a "thingometer."
>
> When the "thingometer" is put to work in the life of Mr. and Mrs. Thing, the result is startling. There he is sitting down on a luxurious and very expensive thing, almost hidden by a large number of other things. Things to sit on, things to sit at, things to cook on, things to eat from, all shining and new. Things, things, things. Things to clean with and things to wash with and things to clean and things to wash. And things to amuse, and things to give pleasure and things to watch and things to play. Things for the long, hot summer and things for the short cold winter. Things for the big thing in which they live and things for the garden and things for the lounge and things for the kitchen and things for the bedroom. And things on four wheels and things on two wheels and things to put on top of the four wheels and things to pull behind the four wheels and things to add to the interior of the things on four wheels. Things, things, things.
>
> And there in the middle are Mr. and Mrs. Thing smiling and pleased pink with things, thinking of more things to add to their things. Secure in their castle of

things. Well Mr. Thing, I have some bad news for you. Oh, you say you cannot hear me because the things are in the way? Well, I just want you to know that your things cannot last. They are going to pass. There's going to be an end to them. Oh, maybe an error in judgment, maybe a temporary loss of concentration, or maybe you'll just pass them off to the secondhand thing dealer. Or maybe they'll wind up a mass of mangled metal being towed off to the thing yard. And what about all the things in your house?

Well, it's time for bed. Put out the cat, make sure you lock the door, to make sure some thing-taker doesn't come and take your things. And that is the way life goes, doesn't it? And some day, when you die, they only put one thing in the box. *You.*

The most important things in life aren't about money or possessions.

Julie and I have found a solution for when we have the urge to buy a lot of things to "have it all." We stop for a minute and list all the things we have to be thankful for. This looking back helps us gain perspective and usually leads to greater contentment. We realize that the most important things in life aren't about money or possessions, but about family, health, friends, relationship with God, and things with eternal value.

As a matter of fact, this reality became very clear to me recently. I was sitting at my computer when all of a sudden I couldn't see some of the words on the screen. I couldn't focus on what I was typing. I tried to focus on some papers on my desk and realized I couldn't read them. Nothing looked right to me! I had jagged vision with a funny light in one eye. At that point my immediate concern was being able to see properly.

"What do I have that I *would not* take money for?"

I have subsequently learned I had an "optical" migraine, which impacts vision. I was relieved that it wasn't more serious and it cleared up quickly. But during those moments of uncertainty, having more and acquiring stuff didn't matter at all. Health superseded all and very quickly gave me a better perspective.

When we're tempted to want more and buy more, we should ask ourselves, "What do I have that I *would not* take money for?" The answer will probably help us realize we're content because most of us have what we need—the basics that really matter. This story by an unknown author drives this point home:

> An American businessman was at the pier of a small coastal village when a small boat with just one fisherman docked. Inside the small boat were several large yellow fin tuna. The American complimented the fisherman on the quality of his fish and asked how long it took to catch them.
>
> The man replied, "Only a little while."
>
> The American then asked why didn't he stay out longer and catch more fish.
>
> The fisherman said he had enough to support his family's immediate needs.
>
> The American then asked, "But what do you do with the rest of your time?"
>
> The fisherman said, "I sleep late, play with my

children, take a siesta with my wife, Maria, stroll into
the village each evening where I sip wine and play guitar with my friends. I have a full and busy life."

The American scoffed. "I have a Harvard MBA,
and I can help you. You should spend more time fishing, and with the proceeds buy a bigger boat. With
the proceeds from the bigger boat, you could buy several boats. Eventually you would have a fleet of fishing
boats. Instead of selling your catch to a middleman,
you would sell directly to the processor, eventually
operating your own cannery. You would control the
product, processing, and distribution. You would need
to leave this small coastal fishing village and move to
Mexico City, then L.A., and eventually New York City,
where you could run your expanding enterprise."

The fisherman asked, "How long would all that take?"

The American replied, "Fifteen to twenty years."

"But what then?"

The American laughed and said, "That's the best
part. When the time is right, you announce an IPO
and sell your company stock to the public and become
very rich. You would make millions."

"Millions? Then what?"

The American said, "Then you could retire. Move
to a small coastal fishing village where you would sleep
late, fish a little, play with your kids, rest with your
wife, and stroll to the village in the evenings where you
could sip wine and play your guitar with your friends!"

Isn't that interesting? The fisherman recognized his needs were
met and he had the important things: spouse, family, and friends.
Many times we already have "it all," but because of the lie of the
world that we always need more, we are missing it.

A vast body of psychological evidence shows that the pleasures of consumption wear off through time and depend heavily on one's frame of reference. Most of us, for instance, occasionally spoil ourselves with outbursts of deliberate and perhaps excessive consumption: a fancy spa treatment, dinner at an expensive restaurant, a shopping spree. In the case of the very wealthy, such forms of consumption can become so commonplace as to lose all psychological benefit: constant luxury is, in a sense, no luxury at all.[5]

Isn't it interesting that the more we buy, the less we enjoy it?

So how about it? Is it time to accept the truth of contentment, count your many blessings, and quit putting your finances on edge by overspending and consuming to have more? I can assure you that this will make your trip through life much more enjoyable.

❧ THINKING IT THROUGH ❧

❏ Have you ever bought something thinking it would really deliver and then it let you down? Explain.

❏ Is there something you really want that, like Scott, if you get it you'll believe you "have arrived"? Explain.

❏ Are you like Danny, who achieved his goals but feels empty when he steps back to look at his life?

❏ Why do you enjoy buying things—really?

❏ Have you had a dramatic experience like Russ momentarily losing part of his sight? How did it affect your outlook on what really matters?

❏ In prayer, do you tend to ask God for more or give thanks for what you already have? If you focus on wants, what does that tell you about yourself? If you focus on giving thanks, how do you maintain that attitude?

8

COMPARISON

"Honey, come on," Bill pleaded while gently tapping on the bathroom door.

"Almost ready," Lori replied. "I just need one more minute."

"Tell me you're not changing again," Bill said. "We need to leave now!"

Suddenly the door opened and Lori burst out. "Okay, I'm ready!" she said, adjusting her dress. "How do I look?"

But Bill had already turned and headed for the door.

Lori scampered to catch up. "I'm trying to look my best, you know. Don't you think the top CPS sales guy deserves the best-looking woman?"

Bill turned to face Lori as he opened the door. "Look, Lori, if I've told you once I've told you a thousand times, you look great in any dress. Now can we just get there?"

When they arrived at the reunion, Bill noticed a few high-powered sports cars in the parking lot. Pulling up and getting out, he didn't say anything, but he refused to look at their family sedan as Lori got out. Together they moved toward the building.

Ten years of marriage, two kids, and several house moves can take a toll on any woman, but a quick scan of the women in the room told Lori she was holding her own against Bill's former classmates. With the exception of one pencil-thin model and a flight attendant who'd never had children, Lori had the flattest stomach at the reunion. *Not bad,* she thought to herself as she watched her husband high-five his college classmates. *Not bad at all.*

The class reunion was a blast, and Bill and Lori were a big-time hit. Snuggling close on the ride home, Lori broke the silence.

"Bill, I was happy to be there with you tonight. I was so proud watching you mingle with all your old friends. You looked as good tonight as the day we were married. I hope I looked that good to you!"

"Lori!" Bill snapped. "How many compliments do you need in one night?"

Sitting up quickly, Lori bit back, "Hey, wait a minute! I work really hard to look good for you. You know that!"

"Yeah—and I've spent a lot of money to keep the look going," Bill returned.

"Well, Mr. Bottom Line, I sure hope it was worth it!" Lori retaliated. "I should have known it would get back to your 'return on investment'! Everything else centers on your ROI. I'm surprised you didn't compare portfolios with your fraternity brothers to see where you are in the standings. Isn't that what really matters to you?"

Bill sat there stunned for a moment. Then he backed off. "I'm sorry, Lori. You're right. I was totally out of line. This isn't about you."

"What is it about then? You've been uptight most of the evening. What's eating you? I know something's not right."

Bill drove silently for a few minutes as he considered Lori's question. "Well, it's hard to explain, but remember Stan, the really tall guy you met when we first got there? He sat with us a while," Bill said.

"Yes, Stan Watson, kind of a geeky guy, single, worked with you at Logan right out of school. What about him?"

"Actually, he worked *for* me," Bill corrected. "Well, once I told Logan I was leaving for sure, they asked if I would help find my replacement. I told them I thought Stan would be great. They agreed and so I trained Stan, and he replaced me when I left."

"Okay. So, what's the rub? You trained the guy, and he's working out great, right?"

"Yes, he's working out. The only reason I left Logan was because CPS had more to offer at the time. It was a step up."

"Plus CPS had me!" Lori interrupted, reminding Bill of where they'd first met.

"I know, I know," Bill said. "Anyway, three months after I left Logan, the company was bought out. That buyout gave the company a huge distribution platform. Two years later, the whole thing went public!"

"Isn't that a good thing?" Lori asked.

"It's a great thing if you're Stan Watson, and you're holding 35,000 stock options. Isn't that just my luck? I take the huge risk and leave Logan, and then Stan, my replacement, cashes in! There's no telling how much that guy is worth now. You know where he lives, don't you? And did you see his car? It was one of those sports cars in the parking lot. Meanwhile, here I am still stuck in the trenches selling software for a living."

"Bill Simpson! You're the top salesman in a growing company. You've got two beautiful children and a wife who loves you. And you're calling that *stuck*?"

Lori's words seemed to vaporize in midair, never reaching their target. Bill was lost in "what could have been."

Comparison

The house is fine—until we visit our neighbor's place. The car is adequate—until we ride in our friend's new two-seater. Our spouses look great—until a great-looking model appears in a commercial. We believe we're doing pretty well—until we meet someone who's doing a little bit better.

Sound familiar? It should. Welcome to the world of comparison.

Comparison is one of those double-edged swords. It's smart to compare alternatives to get the facts. Assessing the similarities and differences of choices allows us to judge and evaluate more effectively. It helps us make better decisions. But when comparison is the grid we use to manage our image or increase our self-worth, we'd better brace ourselves. Comparison is a game we can never win.

When we compare down, we puff ourselves up, enjoying a short-but-exhilarating ride to the top. Then good ol' pride eats us alive.

> Comparison is the archenemy
> of personal contentment.

When we compare up, we feel defeated. Looking at the positive achievements of others can blind us to our own uniqueness, causing us to miss out on how God could be using us for His glory and purpose. And the real tragedy is that comparing ourselves to anyone for any reason will eventually bury us spiritually.

Comparison is the archenemy of personal contentment. Bill and Lori fell prey to the comparison trap. In Bill's eyes, Stan was worth more. The fact that Bill had a family who loved him didn't even factor into his equation. Lori evaluated herself through the lens of physical appearance. Compared to the women at the class reunion, she was on top of the pile. But her view will probably quickly change when she goes to the neighborhood gym and sees the shapely women there. The end result is that Bill and Lori both miss out on enjoying what they already have.

> Comparing ourselves to other people
> never changes reality. It only distorts it.

How can we keep from buying into the comparison lie? By believing the truth. Have you met a person who can say something so cleverly that you didn't realize he or she was talking about you? What do we mean? Well, the apostle Paul says:

> We are not bold to class or compare ourselves with some of those who commend themselves; but when they measure themselves by themselves and compare themselves with themselves, they are without understanding (2 Corinthians 10:12).

At first glance this verse sounds like a tongue twister that seems to be heading in spiritual circles. It's not. It cuts right to the chase. Personal comparison is a bad idea. It will only give us what we *thought* we wanted. Paul is talking about people who are caught up in comparing themselves spiritually. He says, "They are without understanding." Notice Paul didn't say that these people lacked intelligence. In fact, they were probably very bright. They were simply using the wrong standard. They used one another as benchmarks for evaluating how they were doing.

All of us are tempted to compare ourselves physically, emotionally, financially, and spiritually. We compare possessions, accomplishments, gifts, and even ministries. The list can be endless. Sometimes comparison makes us feel better. Other times it makes us feel worse. It all depends on which direction we're stretching the tape. But people make terrible yardsticks. And comparing ourselves to other people never changes reality. It only distorts it. And that is especially true in the area of finances.

Why is it so easy to fall into comparison mode in the arena of finances? Because we have bought into the lie that money, and the things it buys, is a measure of our worth. It's sad, but true. We tend to feel good about ourselves in direct proportion to our financial statement and possessions.

The Lie: "Money and the things it buys are a measure of my self-worth."

One of the first things we ask when we meet somebody is "What do you do?" Or we inquire about someone, "What is he worth?" We're constantly measuring ourselves against others financially to determine how we stack up. Even when we don't want to, our minds have been conditioned to default to these mental gymnastics.

We believe our worthiness is based on our financial statement, what we drive, and where we live. We ascribe value to vocations that generate the most income and less value to lower-paying vocations.

Because we're tempted and encouraged to believe this lie, it's easy to get out of balance as we pursue more and more to feel worthy. We fall into the snare of working longer and harder to have more. One antidote to this constant rushing, striving, stress, and lack of balance in the pursuit of more is to know the truth about money as it relates to our self-worth: Money has nothing to do with our value. Our worth is very clear in Scripture:

The Truth: "What is man that You take thought of him, and the son of man that

> **You care for him? Yet You have made him a**
> **little lower than God, and You crown him**
> **with glory and majesty! You make him to**
> **rule over the works of Your hands; You have**
> **put all things under his feet" (Psalm 8:4-6).**

There are many verses that confirm this very basic, transformational fact about our self-worth. *We're valuable because God says we are valuable!* We have self-worth because God gives us worth.

Interestingly enough, in Psalm 8, David makes this point by using the right kind of comparison. Do we want to know where we are on the ledger? Want to know why we are even on God's mind? Let's see now, David says here's where we fall. We've been made "a little lower than God." Now I don't know about you, but that makes me stop and rethink my value.

In the New Testament we are referred to as God's workmanship, hand-fashioned by Him (Ephesians 2:10). We also see the ultimate expression of our worth to Him in John 3:16, in that God sent His Son to die for us. And if that's not enough, in Genesis 1:26-27 we see God, the Creator of the universe, considering man of such value and worth that He created him in His own image and according to His likeness. We are worth an incredible amount to God regardless of what our financial statements say. This brings to mind a story of an old minister...

> An old minister unwittingly told of his wealth and fortune, and the fame of his possessions got to the ears of the tax assessor. One day the government's representative came to his door to press him for a statement of his wealth.
>
> "Is it so," began the assessor, "that you have capital?"
> "Yes," said the minister. "I am a rich man."
> "In that case," said the visitor interestedly, pulling

out his book, "I shall have to assess you. What are your possessions?"

"I am enjoying good health," said the man, "and good health is worth more than diamonds."

"Congratulations," replied the tax collector, "but don't you own more?"

"Yes! I have healthy, intelligent, upright sons and daughters, and they are possessions of which any man can feel rich."

"Do you own anything else?" asked the government agent.

"Yes, I own citizenship in the United States and an assured inheritance in heaven. What more could a man want?"

"But don't you own money or real estate?"

"No, other than what I've said, I have nothing," said the man happily.

"My friend," the assessor said as he closed his book, "you are indeed a rich man, and your riches are such that no man can take them away—not even the government."

Here are a few more scriptures that really bring home the point that our self-worth is not tied to our money:

You shall remember the LORD your God, for it is He who is giving you power to make wealth (Deuteronomy 8:18).

The rich and the poor have a common bond, the LORD is the maker of them all (Proverbs 22:2).

If God makes both the rich and the poor, then money—or lack of it—can't be a measure of worth. What you and I have financially is mostly a function of our vocations, and our vocations are a result of our giftedness by God. God has gifted each one of us to perform the myriad of jobs that need to be done on this earth. And most of them generate different incomes. Therefore, it follows that what we make is determined by God's calling and the gifts and talents He has given us. Our vocations are not true measures of our self-worth.

If the first antidote to succumbing to comparison is to know the truth about what God says about us, a second antidote is for you and me to keep proper focus and perspective. What does this mean? Keep a *vertical* focus instead of a *horizontal* focus. It's tough to compare ourselves with others if we're not looking horizontally. Feeling a little behind or left out lately? This kind of thinking happens. As a matter of fact, it will always happen when our eyes focus on the people next to us instead of God.

> Our value, our merit, our excellence has
> nothing to do with money, possessions, or net
> worth. It has everything to do with who we
> are in Christ and what God says about us.

Perhaps you didn't win the award at work or you just got passed over for another promotion. Or maybe you're wondering where folding laundry fits into the exciting life your friends are living? Maybe you're wondering why the church never calls to thank you for your service. Maybe you're just plain tired of your old car and small house and don't understand why your neighbors don't seem to struggle like you do. You're wondering why your friends' children seem to win all the awards and are perfect students. You wonder when you can upgrade your house or get that cabin at the lake. And what about some new clothes? Someone in the crowd (in your peripheral, horizontal vision) will always be "in" or have more. That, however, should never keep you from feeling worthy. You *are,* and it has nothing to do with money.

I understand this challenge to avoid comparison. When Julie and I first lived in Atlanta, we moved into an apartment. We were on the affluent side of town, and it didn't take long for us to observe all the nice houses that many of our church friends lived in. I remember the dialogue about how nice it would be to have a house and "how can these folks afford all those nice things?" As we noted earlier, many people have stuff that isn't paid for and are really in a house of cards built on debt. Still, this didn't keep us from some covetous thoughts and some "why not us, God?" discussions.

When these discussions began, Julie and I asked the question highlighted in the last chapter: *What do we have that we would not take money for?* This helped us gain perspective and clarify what was really important to us. This question is a great one to ask anytime we start to feel like we got the short end of the stick financially. I've worked with multimillionaires with whom I would not trade places for any amount of money. They have the money, but their family lives, marriages, and other relational issues are challenging. Gaining proper perspective and keeping a vertical focus will help us curb our appetites when we're tempted to overspend to keep up.

In summary, our value, our merit, our excellence has nothing to do with money, possessions, or net worth. It has everything to do with who we are in Christ and what God says about us.

You and I have a choice. We can measure ourselves with what God says or what the world says. We can either believe the lie that somehow our net worth is equal to our self-worth or the truth that our relationship with God determines our worth.

Putting Non-comparison into Practice

Now, it's time to be really honest. The advice Kelly and I have just offered is hard to implement. We live in a culture that values appearance over character. And when we stop to think about it, that focus really hasn't changed since the beginning of time.

When Samuel went to select a new king for Israel, the first thing he did was look at the appearance of Jesse's boys. Surely one of them would be king! But in 1 Samuel 16:7 we read, "The LORD said to Samuel, 'Do not look at his appearance or at the height of his stature, because I have rejected him; for God sees not as man sees, for man looks at the outward appearance, but the LORD looks at the heart.'" So there you have it. God is more concerned about your heart and walk with Him than anything you own or wear.

So isn't it time to acknowledge who you are in Christ and quit comparing? Comparing isn't wise. In fact, it borders on stupidity. It can even lead to making dumb financial decisions.

The only person the apostle Paul compared himself with was the Lord. That is the proper plumb line. Which tape are you measuring with?

❧ THINKING IT THROUGH ❧

❏ Is comparison an issue for you? Why or why not?

❏ In the area of money, do you tend to compare up, down, or both?

❏ Which of these blanks did you most recently fill in mentally:

"I'm doing better than _____."

"I'm not doing as well as _____."

❏ Do you tend to tie your worth to your bank account?

❏ Do you feel pressured to get out of balance and accumulate more?

❏ Do you think others know when you're using them as a yardstick?

❏ What's the *truth* about money and your self-worth?

9

IOU

Mike Baxter was a successful financial planner with a strong family legacy. His grandfather was a brilliant physician and pillar of the community. His dad was a gifted pastor who led the city's most vibrant church. Both were role models who imparted wisdom through their many popular sayings and quotes. This was a Baxter tradition. All of those sayings inspired Mike, but none meant more than his grandfather's favorite:

> Know what you owe, and to whom it's due.
> Then make it a point to see payment through.

In his early days as a planner, Mike used that saying to encourage his clients to pay their debts quickly. Over time he applied it to more than just clearing the books.

For Mike Baxter, The Curb Diner was the perfect place to enjoy a good meal. Great food and personal service were just the tip of the iceberg. Mike's table by the window gave him a birds-eye view of the most colorful intersection in town. It was a great spot to meet with clients or park there alone to completely escape. On days like today, Mike would sit mesmerized by people streaming by, inches away from his private world.

"Here you go, Mr. Baxter," the cheerful waitress announced. "One decaf, double-cap, semidry with extra foam! Will anyone be joining you today, or will you be staring out that window all by yourself?"

Mike snapped out of it. "Oh…thank you, Ashley. I guess I was daydreaming!"

His daughter's best friend flashed a big smile as she placed the coffee on the table.

"I guess so! Now, what'll it be, one menu or two?"

"Two menus, Ashley. Rusty Duncan will be joining me shortly."

"Rusty Duncan!" Ashley beamed. "Nice work, Mr. Baxter! Nice work indeed!"

"You know Rusty?" Mike asked with surprise.

"Come on, Mr. Baxter! What single girl doesn't know about Mr. Aviation? The guy is hot!"

"I thought he was cool," Mike responded as he reached for the menu.

"Hot is cool and cool is hot, Mr. Baxter. Don't worry, you'll catch up," Ashley chirped with a grin.

"Don't count on it," Mike said. "So what's the special today?"

"Well, it's Wednesday, so you should know. But just in case, here you go. Wednesday means…"

Mike held up his hand and finished her sentence, "Pork chops and greens."

"You've got it!" Ashley affirmed with a solid high-five. "Now, when the flyboy lands, please tell him about the special. Meanwhile, I'll be in the back checking my face."

Mike laughed out loud. "Thanks, Ashley. Run along and do what you do."

As Ashley turned to leave, Mike added, "Oh, one more thing…"

"What's that?" Ashley asked, looking back.

"Did I ever tell you that you're the best?"

"Every time you come in!" Ashley said. "Every time you come in."

Ashley Mason was the biggest reason Mike Baxter came to The Curb. Two years earlier, she wasn't just his daughter Michelle's best friend—she was her only friend. When no one could get through to Michelle, Ashley had her ear. When everyone wanted to give up on Michelle, Ashley wouldn't. And when Michelle finally decided to reach out for help, Ashley was there to take her hand. As he watched this vibrant young lady work her way across the room, Mike quietly gave thanks. He owed Ashley everything. Coming to The Curb was one small way he could "see his payment through." Then he caught sight of Rusty and smiled as he thought about their meeting. *Working with someone's personal finances is a lot like a doctor reading an MRI,* he decided. *It's a rare peek inside. It illuminates the unseen.*

Much like his granddad viewed his patients and his dad looked at his congregation, Mike viewed his clients as a sacred trust. They were sent to him for a purpose. He knew that his financial advice wasn't just for that moment in time. It could and would affect generations to come. Mike loved what he did because it counted for eternity. And the part of his job he loved the most—a chance to serve—had just walked through the restaurant's front door.

Rusty Duncan was a second-generation entrepreneur who'd inherited a thriving aviation business when cancer took his father, Mack, home to be with the Lord. Mack had been a client and friend of Mike's. Now Mike welcomed every opportunity to be here for Rusty.

Rusty had grown up at the local airport. His mom answered the phones and kept the books while his dad bought and sold and repaired small planes. Rusty was a natural pilot. His dad taught him to fly before he could drive. Taking over for Mack wasn't easy for Rusty, but it was shaping him into a man his dad would have been proud of.

Rusty approached Mike with a smile and extended hand. "Great to see you, Mr. Baxter."

"You keep that hand, son. I'll take a hug," Mike said emphatically as he rose.

The two hugged warmly and took their seats.

Rusty began the dialogue immediately. "First, I want to apologize for the short notice. I know how busy you are, sir, and what a chore it is to…"

Mike flashed the time out sign, stopping Rusty mid-sentence.

"Pop quiz, son. Answer correctly and you'll win a free lunch. Ready?"

Rusty nodded as if he knew what was coming.

Holding up one finger, Mike proceeded. "What's the one promise I made to your dad?"

Rusty cracked a smile and looked down briefly. "I think it was something like 'I promise I'll never be too busy to meet with your son.'"

Leaning forward, Mike continued, "That's a promise I intend to keep. It's never a chore to meet with you. And after three years of watching you grow up, I can honestly say it's a privilege! Now let that sink in, and then tell me what's on your mind."

Rusty nodded gratefully. "I really don't know how to lay this out, Mr. Baxter. You know how careful I've tried to be with everything Dad left us. And for the most part I think I've done a pretty good job."

"A great job!" Mike added.

"Thank you, sir." Rusty responded. "Well, I thought it would get easier, but it hasn't. I'm glad we're growing, but there are so many things that hit me day to day. I can't seem to keep track of them all. And frankly, Mr. Baxter, my mom hasn't been the same since Dad passed. She seems to be making more mistakes lately."

Mike nodded. "We've talked about this before, Rusty. Your mom needs time away from the shop. She may even be in a little over her head. Would you like me to come out and talk to her?"

Rusty didn't answer. Instead he reached for his briefcase, removed a thin blue folder, and handed it to Mike. Mike opened the folder to find two sheets of figures and a coupon for taxes due to the IRS—all came from Rusty's accountant.

"Do we have a tax issue, Rusty?" Mike asked as he focused on the letter.

"Well, we've got some kind of issue," Rusty responded. "Check it out, Mr. Baxter. They say I owe them 50 grand!"

As Mike read the letter, he heard a familiar voice.

"Good afternoon," Ashley announced as she brought Rusty a glass of water. "My name is Ashley, and I'll be taking care of you today."

"Good afternoon," Rusty answered politely.

Ashley pointed toward Mike. "Did Mr. Baxter tell you about the special or would you like me to fill you in?"

Sensing he was alone for the moment, Rusty replied, "He didn't tell me anything yet. Can you give us a few minutes before we order?"

"Not a problem!" Ashley affirmed with a smile. "Look over the menu. The specials are on the back. Just flag me when you two get hungry."

"Will do," Rusty acknowledged.

After poring over the letter, Mike turned to the financial sheets. Noticing they were identical, he handed one to Rusty without looking up.

"What do you think, Mr. Baxter?" Rusty asked nervously. "That letter is pretty strong, isn't it? I'll tell you right now, I can't write a check for $50,000!"

Mike was making his second pass over the sheet and had yet to look up.

"Well, Mr. Baxter, what do you think?" Rusty asked again.

"Well," Mike said calmly, "it appears you owe the government some money."

"It can't be that much, though!" Rusty shot back.

"And why is that, Rusty?" Mike asked.

"Because I don't have that much. It's as simple as that!"

Mike waited to see if Rusty would continue. It didn't take long.

"Look, Mr. Baxter. You know how careful we are. Mom and I watch every dime, and I never spend money foolishly. But the government makes it nearly impossible to run a business. I pay quarterly tax estimates, and Mom always seems to be writing tax checks. We send them all year long, and at the end of the year they want more! If I spend time trying to dispute it, the number goes up. They're relentless. I can see why so many people go out of business. The government forces them out. We can't keep up, and we don't even have debt! Taxes are our biggest problem."

Mike took a sip of his coffee and picked up the numbers sheet. "Rusty, I think we have two separate issues here. One is what the letter says. The other is why you got the letter in the first place."

Rusty was puzzled. "With all due respect, sir, that doesn't make sense. I know what the letter says, and I know why I got it!"

"Okay, why do you think you got the letter?" Mike asked evenly.

Rusty tried to appear just as calm. "I got the letter because the government wants another $50,000. They are sticking it to me. Isn't that it in a nutshell?"

"No, not exactly," Mike replied.

Rusty grabbed the letter and stared at it. "Well, I'm looking at a letter addressed to me, and it says right here in caps: PLEASE REMIT $50,000. LOVE AND KISSES. THE IRS!"

Rusty was on the ledge, and Mike knew it. He decided to be gentle but direct.

"Rusty, I want you to forget about that letter for a minute, okay?"

"What do you mean forget about it? That's why I came here!" Rusty huffed.

"Trust me, son. Put the letter aside for a moment and pick up that sheet of numbers. The one showing the company's profit and loss for the past two years."

Reluctantly, Rusty obeyed. "Okay."

"This sheet compares your revenue, expenses, and net income in the business for the past two years," Mike said.

"So?" retorted Rusty. "What's the big deal?"

"Tell me about the first three lines. These are your three sources of revenue, right?"

"Yes, sir. The first line is fuel sales, the second is repairs, and the third is aircraft sales. Notice they're all up right now, especially aircraft sales!" Rusty said proudly.

"I see that!" Mike agreed. "You sold what…14 planes last year?"

"Sixteen!" Rusty corrected. "First time we've ever sold four planes, four quarters straight."

"Congratulations! Your dad would be proud of you," Mike said.

"Not if he saw that IRS letter!" Rusty mumbled.

"What letter?" Mike said pointedly, pausing before he continued. "So let's see. You had revenue of 2 million compared to 1.5 million the year before. That's great growth, Rusty," Mike said with an encouraging smile.

"Yes, sir." Rusty agreed. "We got a great price on the planes we sold, and we bought fuel in bulk at a low price point. We've had the best year since Dad died, and I've finally been able to take some decent money out of the business."

"I see," Mike said as he studied the sheet. "Revenue is certainly up in all three of your profit centers, that's for sure."

"With sales up, we had more cash. We haven't needed to use our credit line in 14 months. No debt, just like you taught me."

"I see there's no debt. That's great! How did you decide how much to take out in salary?" Mike asked.

Rusty thought back. "Mr. Baxter, I didn't take any more salary than I did last year: $6000 a month." Rusty paused. "Hmmm… come to think of it, I did take a few extra draws when Mom told me how much cash we had accumulating in the bank. I needed to fix up the house. You know how bachelor pads can get. I also bought a new Lexus. Our clients expect us to look successful."

Mike was beginning to see the issue. "Any other big-ticket items?"

"Well, there was the new Jet Ski. With all the activity at the business, I needed to unwind. But you will be proud of me! I paid cash for everything—the remodeling, the car, and the Jet Ski."

"So how much extra *did* you draw out?" Mike asked.

Rusty did some mental gymnastics. "I guess about $130,000 to $140,000."

Mike paused to let this amount sink in to Rusty's consciousness. "Did you pay quarterly estimates on your salary and your extra draws…or just the salary?"

"Just the salary. Doesn't the business pay taxes on my draws since they were extra profits from our good year?" Rusty asked. "Taxes on my salary, more taxes to the state, taxes on my draws, and taxes on my business profits. How is a guy ever going to get ahead?" Rusty continued with frustration. "I liked it better when I was poorer!"

"Well, Rusty, don't hit me when I say this, but taxes are a good thing. They are an indicator of your financial success," Mike responded seriously.

"Well, if I have any more success it will break the bank!"

Did you catch the money problem in the story?

The Lie: "Taxes are my biggest problem."

One of the hardest things to come to grips with, whether you own your business or work for someone else, is that the tax collector is faithfully standing at the door wanting to be paid. The IRS wants its money when you make it. And the more you make, the more it takes from you. And that's what we should expect.

> **The Truth: "Give to everyone what you owe them: If you owe taxes, pay taxes; if revenue, then revenue; if respect, then respect; if honor; then honor"** (Romans 13:7 NIV).

Rusty's story isn't unusual. Just when we think we're getting ahead with our business...or we get a raise...or a bonus, our joy is shattered by the tax bill. Sadly, we always seem to realize we've jumped up in tax brackets *after* we've spent our newfound money.

Taxes Are Not the Problem

Rusty didn't really have a tax problem. Rusty had an *ownership* problem. He forgot that the government *owns* a portion of our money. Why did Rusty have a hard time paying the IRS bill? He hadn't planned well. This is a common mistake many of us make. We unknowingly spend what is not ours.

What do I mean by that? On every dollar we earn, we owe state (unless you're in one of the few states where there is no state tax), federal, and Social Security taxes. So we really don't have a dollar to spend when we earn a dollar.

I recently helped one of my married sons work through how to figure out what he had available for living expenses. Maybe this will help you too.

First, I had him take his prior year tax return and add up the three tax totals (state, federal, and Social Security).

Second, I had him divide that number by his total earned income for that year. This resulted in a percentage that represented his *effective tax rate*. Effective tax rate is the percent of every dollar earned that goes to taxes.[1]

In my son's case, 18 percent went to taxes. Therefore, he has 82 cents from every dollar to spend for living, giving, and debt payments, in addition to any savings he wants to set aside.

This is what Rusty forgot to figure into his spending. Even though the company made more money and the cash was in the bank, he should have been figuring what his "after tax" amount was. It appears he was in a 30 percent-plus effective rate based on his tax bill. He really only had about $100,000 to spend, not the $130,000 to $140,000 he thought he had. And not having the money on hand didn't mean he didn't owe the IRS $50,000.

Unfortunately, I get a lot of clients in Rusty's situation. Business owners who were required to pay estimates quarterly, and, in many cases, didn't increase their tax deposits when their income increased. Kelly fell into this category. When I first met him he was a landscaper (a sole proprietor). He told me he could live on $35,000 a year. I told him he could not. The real number was more like $50,000 because he wasn't allowing for the taxes he would owe each April. Sure enough the tax bill would come, and he didn't have the cash on hand to pay the IRS.

It's easier to get in a bind if you're in business for yourself and don't have the taxes being withheld than if you're an employee with only W-2 wages. However, even if you're employed somewhere and your taxes are withheld, you can still get a surprise when dividends, stock sales, and other sources of income not from your employer are added in. No one can spend 100 percent of every dollar he or she takes in from any source because of taxes owed.

Beware of Tax Shelters

Another observation based on experience is that people will do everything they can to avoid paying taxes. In the early years of our business (the 1980s) "tax shelters" were the rage. Most tax shelters were real estate related, but we also saw oil deals, Arabian horse deals, barge deals, cattle breeding deals, and on and on. People focused on the upfront tax savings rather than the true economics of the deal. In more cases than not, not only did the investors lose their entire investments, but the upfront tax savings were eventually recaptured by the IRS. They lost on both counts.

Fortunately, over the past couple of decades, most of these tax loopholes have been closed. That's good because we've found that the temptation to look for investments and programs to avoid paying taxes often leads to unwise decisions.

Don't make crazy investments
in an effort to avoid taxes.

You Want to Pay Tax

"I want to pay taxes? You've got to be kidding, Russ!" you say. "Why would I *want* to pay taxes?" Two reasons. First, the only reason you owe taxes is because you had income. You made money! We don't owe taxes if we haven't made any money. And more taxes are an indicator of financial success. This is what Mike was trying to get Rusty to see. The second reason you want to pay taxes is out of obedience to God's Word: "If you owe taxes, pay taxes" (Romans 13:7). Taxes provide government (the civil authority over us) the funds for the infrastructure we enjoy: roads, air traffic control, military protection, national parks, food safety, and so forth. I don't like to pay taxes any more than the next person, but it helps ease the pain when I realize the benefits I enjoy in this country because of the taxes I pay.

Yes, we should be good stewards and handle our money wisely. That means taking advantage of legitimate tax-saving investments. Don't let the "tax tail wag the dog." This means don't make crazy investments in an effort to avoid taxes. If you have a positive margin after living expenses, giving, and paying your taxes, then making tax-advantaged investments such as a 401(k) plan is a good idea. Retirement plans defer taxes and offer tax-advantaged growth until withdrawal.

Remember, you can only pay off debt or accumulate cash with *after-tax* dollars.

Second, I want to pay taxes because *not* being able to pay taxes is often a symptom of a "living expense" or debt problem. I have people like Rusty tell me all the time that if they didn't owe so much in taxes, they would be okay. After asking questions to get the facts, I can usually determine what could be the root cause of the problem. If they say the $30,000 in taxes they pay is killing them, I calmly point out that the reason they owe this amount is because they made $95,000. And the reason they needed to make that much is because they needed $60,000 to live on. Taxes are a function of lifestyle. Lifestyle drives your income need, and the more income you make, the higher your taxes.

Another point to understand is that you can only pay off debt or accumulate cash for savings or an emergency fund with *after-tax* dollars. What does this mean? This means you have to earn the money, pay the taxes, and then you can pay off debt or save. So to get out of debt and accumulate cash you will have to pay taxes first. There's no other way to do it without getting into financial trouble.

Also, there are things worse than taxes. I like this quote by Benjamin Franklin:

> Friends and neighbors complain that taxes are indeed very heavy, and if those laid on by the government were the only ones we had to pay, we might the more easily discharge them; but we have many other, and much more grievous to some of us. We are taxed twice as much by our idleness, three times as much by our pride, and four times as much by our folly.

Idleness, pride, and folly are worse than taxes.

In summary, plan for your taxes and look at taxes as a blessing. Contrary to what Rusty thinks, paying taxes will not break him, but taking draws out of the business without paying the taxes along the way will. Rusty had overlooked the blessing that the taxes were showcasing—his business was prospering and he was making money.

⊰ THINKING IT THROUGH ⊱

❑ Why is it so difficult to think positively when it comes to taxes?

❑ Do you know your "effective tax rate"?

❑ What should Rusty have done differently to ease his tax burden?

❑ Do you typically get a tax refund or do you owe taxes?

10

GIVING IT UP

When Chip Raines paused and gripped the edge of the pulpit, his congregation knew he was fighting back tears of joy. Five years earlier, Chip had arrived with a vision to plant a new kind of church. He had shared that dream everywhere he went. And even though his heart for God was evident and his vision was extremely compelling, few believed he would succeed. But Chip's philosophy was simple: *Since God didn't hold anything back, neither would he.*

Chip's love for God and his vision were contagious. What began as a seven-couple Bible study quickly grew into a vibrant congregation. Big Creek Community Church was now a congregation of more than 500 people! The church had quickly outgrown the school gymnasium where they first met. Now they faced the challenge of hiring new staff.

"This is one of the biggest moments in Big Creek's history," Chip said slowly. "In the past five years we've seen God do what some thought was impossible. And though it's been so hard at times, I can't imagine doing anything else with my life."

The congregation erupted into a burst of applause, and when

it did, Chip broke down. Gathering himself, Chip continued. "You've all sacrificed so much. You've given your time, you've shared your talents, and you've invested your hard-earned money to get us where we are today. Our debt-free policy allows us to operate with an incredible freedom that will enable us to have more ministry than ever before. As we move into our new fiscal year, we're asking God to enlarge our borders and give us the funds to increase our staff. With a budget increase of $100,000, we will be able to double our children's ministry, expand our high school footprint, and give more to missions. At this time I'm going to ask the ushers to come forward to collect the general fund pledges for the year. May God richly bless the sacrifice we're about to make for Him!"

Phil and Wendy were new to Big Creek. They'd been invited by their landlord only months before. They were fairly new Christians who'd moved to town when Phil was offered a company job change. They loved the people of the church and enjoyed Chip's messages, but Phil felt overwhelmed with the idea of giving his money to support the church.

"What's wrong, Phil?" Wendy asked on the way home. "You haven't said a word since we came out of church."

"I don't know what it is," Phil said flatly.

"Come on, Phil. You *do* know what it is," Wendy insisted. "You're upset about the budget increase, aren't you?"

"It's not the budget," Phil responded. "I guess every church needs a budget. But that's all we talk about. It's like money is the only thing that matters around here."

"No, it's not," Wendy said with a smile. "You have to realize that we've only been here for a few months. These people have been building something for several years now. It's just a season, Phil. Once we get the staff we need, this will be behind us."

"That's what they say, but you know that's not true. Building a church is like building a house. It never stops. The more people that come, the more money it costs to run the place. It'll never end!" Phil said emphatically.

"Well, that may be true. But as the church grows, there will be more people to help out," Wendy said encouragingly.

"Now you're starting to sound like them," Chip snapped.

"What do you mean *them*?" Wendy asked with surprise. "I thought this was *our* church. I thought this was 'us,' not 'them.'"

"Honestly, Wendy," Phil shot back. "It irritates me to hear things like 'for only 100 grand!' Really, Pastor Chip? Is that all? The guy says 100 grand like it's nothing. That's more than I'll make in two years! Does he think I'm made of money?"

"It's all relative, Phil. In the big scheme of things, it's really not that much money," Wendy said. "Besides, Chip didn't ask us to give it all. He just asked us to do our part. And that's what we did. We prayed about it and did our part, right?"

Phil didn't say a word. He just stared straight ahead and bit his lip.

Wendy tried to get his attention. "Earth to Phil, your wife's calling!"

Phil didn't come close to responding.

"Phil, wake up!" Wendy said with a nudge. "Now you're being stubborn!"

Phil looked over. "Stubborn about what?"

"Well, I left off with, 'we did our part, right?'" Wendy replied.

"I know where you left off," Phil snapped again, focusing back on the road.

"So?" Wendy asked.

"So what?" Phil said.

"Phil, look at me!" Wendy demanded just as they stopped at a stop sign.

Phil refused to look at her.

"Okay, don't look at me." Wendy added, "But if you won't look at me, then at least tell me one thing."

"What?" Phil asked without changing his tone.

"Tell me that we did our part," Wendy said.

After a long hesitation, Phil responded. "I really can't say that we did, Wendy."

"What do you mean you can't say that we did?" Wendy asked. "We prayed about it together, and we decided on an amount. I wrote the check and you put it in the pledge envelope. So what's the problem?"

"The problem is this," Phil said. He reached for his Bible and handed it to Wendy.

"The Bible?" Wendy asked. "The problem is the Bible? That makes no sense at all!"

"Open it," Phil said.

"To what?" Wendy asked.

"Just open it," Phil answered.

Wendy opened Phil's Bible and found the yellow pledge envelope stuck in the middle.

"No way!" Wendy said, shocked. "You didn't turn this in!"

"I just couldn't do it," Phil said. "I just started this new job, and we're barely making ends meet now."

"We're fine!" Wendy objected. "We're fine and I'm not even working yet. I'm so disappointed in you. You hold on to money like you'll have it forever. We prayed about this, Philip! Doesn't that mean anything to you?"

"Look, you and I are saving for a house. We'll never get a house of our own if we keep giving so much to the church. I take care of the money, and trust me when I say this: We can't afford to give right now!"

THE LIE: "I can't afford to give."

How many of us are like Phil? We can't seem to give what we would like to or what people expect us to. We've all been here at some point. I've been in the business of helping people increase their giving for more than 30 years. I've found that like other financial issues, the subject of giving more means different things for different people. Some of our clients are always looking for ways to maximize their giving. Others struggle with setting and reaching a specific tithe level. Another observation is that human nature can be very creative when it comes to thinking of "why not to give" excuses.

Let's attack this issue systematically. First, we'll look at a few reasons people feel they can't afford to give. We will then look at some reasons why we can't afford *not* to give."

Why We Feel We Can't Afford to Give

Not having enough. It's natural to fear we won't have enough to meet our needs if we give some of our money away. Aren't we supposed to have an emergency fund, buy a house, provide food and clothing, and pay the utility bills? Like Phil told Wendy, it's tough enough to make ends meet without giving money away. On top of current needs, there are funds needed for education and, eventually, retirement. After all, we can't expect the government to provide all we need for our retirement years. If we're to provide for our families in all of these areas, then giving money away seems contrary to our goals.

We rationalize that we'll give after we have taken care of (or at least gotten a good head start on) all of these other things. What happens, in reality, is that all other uses of money—living, taxes, debt, and investments—take first priority. The result? There is rarely any money left to give. Instead of giving from our "first-fruits," as Scripture tells us, God gets the leftovers (which usually aren't there).

Lack of giving role models. We might not give because we've never seen financial generosity modeled. I fell into this trap. We attended a small country church during my childhood, and when it came to giving, all I ever saw happen was a couple of dollars dropped in the offering plate as it was passed down the pews. I didn't see financial generosity, so I had no context for what it meant to give liberally.

Then I met Julie. I joke with people that my wife didn't bring any debt into our marriage, but she sure did bring in charitable support obligations for people all around the country. I used to quiz her: "What is this organization? Who are these people? Why are we sending them money?" She'd calmly point out that they were Campus Crusade for Christ missionaries that she had been supporting as part of her giving. This was a new concept for me. I had never really given much of anything to the church, other charities, or people. Julie's example caused me to pause and consider this "giving idea" as a normal use of some of the money flowing through our hands.

Not understanding Scripture. The third reason we think we can't afford to give is that we don't know what God's Word says about giving. This applied to me. I came to Christ at age 13, and not only had I not seen giving modeled, I really didn't know what the Bible taught about the subject. When I went to work for Ronald Blue & Co. that changed. I quickly learned the New Testament had more to say about money than about heaven and hell combined. And much of that financial instruction was about giving. (Our purpose in this book isn't to unpack all of what the Bible says about giving, but we've provided a list of recommended reading in the back if you want to delve deeper into this topic.)

All of us are commanded to give, and if we want to be obedient, then not giving *is not* an option for Christians. The commandment to give seems to fall into the "suggestion category" for many believers. That's another lie dispelled by Scripture.

Why We Can't Afford *Not* to Give

Yes, we can make excuses about not being able to afford to give, but are we missing something far more important than money when we don't give? Yes! We could be missing God's blessing.

> THE TRUTH: "Give, and it will be given to you. A good measure, pressed down, shaken together and running over, will be poured into your lap. For with the measure you use, it will be measured to you" (Luke 6:38 NIV).

This good measure includes freedom, a secure investment, and a solid foundation.

Giving leads to freedom. The premise for this book is that God's truth for managing money is different than what the world propagates. We want you to "know the truth, and the truth will set you free" (John 8:32). Luke 16:13 clearly states our dilemma when it comes to experiencing freedom: "No servant can serve two masters; for either he will hate the one and love the other, or else he will be devoted to one and despise the other. You cannot serve God and wealth [money]."

Jesus could have listed any number of subjects in juxtaposition to serving God. He could have said God and *power,* or God and *prestige,* or God and *creation.* But He didn't. He said God and *money.* Why? Because money is the one thing in our lives that we feel can give us all the things we want (and that God wants to give us)—security, provision, power, contentment, self-worth, identity, and so forth. Luke 16:12 does not suggest that we *might* be able to serve God and wealth. It says we *cannot.* No wiggle room! It's *impossible* to serve both! So how do we make sure God—and not money—is on the throne of our lives? *We give.* A disciplined pattern of giving regularly breaks the power of money because giving becomes a natural and vital part of our lives.

The best way to illustrate this truth is the monkey and the jar. The story says that trappers found the best way to catch a monkey was to take a jar with a narrow neck, put a fig inside, and then put the jar inside a cage. The monkey would come along, reach inside the cage, and put his hand into the jar to grab the fig. When he tried to pull his hand out he couldn't get it out unless he let go of the fig, which he would not do. He was trapped because the jar wouldn't fit through the bars!

And that's the same with us. If we hold on to our money with a closed fist, it traps us. It becomes our focus, our sense of identity, our worth. Only when we open our hands and loosen our grip will we become free. How about your hand? Is it open or closed?

In the third century, Cyprian, bishop of Carthage, wrote this description of the affluent:

> Their property held them in chains...chains which shackled their courage and choked their faith and hampered their judgment and throttled their souls...They think of themselves as owners, whereas it is they rather who are owned: enslaved as they are to their own property, they are not the masters of their money but its slaves.

As Cyprian noted, if we don't give, we're acting as if we really own our money. That's not the case. *God owns it.* What do we have that we were not given? (See 1 Corinthians 4:7.) The cattle on a thousand hills are God's, along with everything that moves in the field (Psalm 50:10-11). The earth and all it contains is His (Psalm 24:1). David understood this clearly. "But who am I and who are my people that we should be able to offer as generously as this? For all things come from You, and from Your hand we have given You" (1 Chronicles 29:14). Giving is a tangible way to acknowledge the ultimate ownership and provision of our sovereign God in our lives.

One last thought about this issue of freedom. As we get free from money, God is free to bless us. If our hands are open, it's easier for Him to put something in them! This doesn't mean that *if* we give, we will always get money in return. But God does work on a reward system as we will soon discover, and it's much better to have open hands than closed ones.

Giving is a wise investment. All of us want to be wise instead of foolish, but how is giving money away wise? Well, for one thing, it shows we have a biblical perspective on what is really going to last in eternity and we're investing accordingly.

Are we storing up treasures in the right place? In Luke 12:16-21, we read the parable of a rich farmer. He had a choice as to what to do with his riches. He could be generous and give or he could store up more for himself. He chose the latter and gets this harsh indictment: "God said to him, 'You fool! This very night your soul is required of you; and now who will own what you have prepared?' So is the man who stores up treasure for himself, and is not rich toward God" (verses 20-21).

Randy Alcorn, in his book *Money, Possessions, and Eternity,* uses a great analogy to illustrate this principle:

> Imagine for a moment that you are alive at the very end of the Civil War. You are living in the South, but home is really in the North. While in the South, you have accumulated a good amount of Confederate currency. Suppose you also know for a fact that the North is going to win the war and that the end could come at any time. What will you do with all of your Confederate money?
>
> If you are smart, there is only one answer to the question. You would cash in your Confederate currency for US currency—the only money that will have value once the war is over. You would keep only enough Confederate currency to meet your basic needs for that short

period until the war was over and the money would become worthless. As believers, we have inside knowledge of an eventual major change in the worldwide social and economic situation. The currency of this world—its money and possessions—will be worthless at our death or at Christ's return, both of which are imminent. This should encourage us to use a lot of our money for eternal purposes.

Matthew 6:19-21 is also clear on where we should store up or invest our money.

> Do not store up for yourselves treasures on earth, where moth and rust destroy, and where thieves break in and steal. But store up for yourselves treasures in heaven, where neither moth nor rust destroys, and where thieves do not break in or steal; for where your treasure is, there your heart will be also.

In light of this truth, if we are wise, we will send money on ahead to store it up in a safe place instead of just storing up more in pension accounts, brokerage accounts, home equity, and such on earth. How do we store up treasure in heaven? We invest in people-oriented endeavors that will encourage them to believe in Jesus Christ and grow in their knowledge of the Word of God. People and the Word of God are the only two things that last forever.

We can give to our local church, missionaries, send teenagers on summer mission projects, help build structures, provide food for the homeless, pay the rent for a needy family, provide for Bible translating, and give to many other worthy projects. Once we open our hands and desire to store up treasure in the right place, God will give us the wisdom as to *how much*, *where*, and *when* to give.

If we know giving allows accumulation of treasure in heaven, why do we often feel like we can't afford to give? To a large degree it's as C.S. Lewis noted: "It is since Christians have largely ceased to think of the other world that they have become so ineffective in this. Aim at Heaven and you will get earth 'thrown in'; aim at earth and you will get neither."[1] We need to keep an eternal perspective, and giving helps us do that.

> When we believe we can't afford
> to give, that is a short-term focus
> that will ultimately result in loss.

Once I began to give and exhibit generosity, it's been neat to see all the opportunities Julie and I have been given to invest. After 30 years of practicing the discipline of giving, it has been—and still is—a lot of fun. Not only have we been blessed to meet needs, but we still have food on the table, money in the bank, funds in retirement accounts, kids' education paid for, and cash to go out to eat every now and then. In my vocation, I have counseled thousands of people and never have I had one of them not be able to afford to give. Maybe not a lot at first, but they could afford to give something to acknowledge God's ownership.

I remember one couple vividly. When they came to us, they said they wanted to be good stewards and diversify their assets. We crafted a plan to help them accomplish these objectives. As part of the plan, we showed them how they could increase their giving 10 times. They implemented this plan, and now almost 30 years later they're doing fine. Now in their eighties, they've given away millions while still having all their needs met. I share this story to illustrate that in *God's economy* we cannot give ourselves broke. We really cannot "out give God," as the saying goes.

I'm not saying we give to get. Quite the contrary. We give

because it's wise and it's commanded by God. When we give, we experience real life because, as Winston Churchill said, "We make a living by what we get—we make a life by what we give."

Giving builds a solid foundation. A final reason we cannot afford *not* to give is that giving is the only way to store up a solid foundation. We all want stability. Especially in uncertain times. I'm writing this book as we continue to recover from the Great Recession of 2008 and uncertainty is fresh on everyone's mind. Everyone seemed surprised when their investment accounts and retirement monies dropped 40 percent in a few short months. They should not have been. First Timothy 6:17-19 gives a clear message about the uncertainty of earthly riches:

> Instruct those who are rich in this present world not to be conceited or to fix their hope on the uncertainty of riches, but on God, who richly supplies us with all things to enjoy. Instruct them to do good, to be rich in good works, to be generous and ready to share, storing up for themselves the treasure of a good foundation for the future, so that they may take hold of that which is life indeed.

That's what's so cool about God. He is very clear, and this verse gives us clarity on several issues relative to our money.

- We are not to be conceited or arrogant about our riches. We have what we have by God's goodness to us. (In chapter 15 we'll look at this in more detail.)

- We are not to put our hope in uncertain riches, but in God. Money and the things it buys are uncertain. Luke 16:9 drives that point home when it says, "when [money] fails." As folks watched their investment accounts plummet in value and their homes lose equity rapidly in the recession, this truth became real. Anxiety and angst replaced hope and confidence. That's what happens when a person's hope or focus is on the wrong thing. We should be more preoccupied with the unchanging character of our sovereign, almighty God rather than the circumstantial evidence of doom all around us. *We need to put our hope in Him and count on His dependability rather than the ominous headlines of impending catastrophe that confront us daily.*

- We are to do good, be rich in good works, and be generous and willing to share. The emphasis needs to be on a *giving* mindset. (This foundation is certain, is in heaven, and is inextricably linked to God's heart.) And here is the real kicker: You and I are rewarded when we give. This storing up is for us! There is profit increasing in my account as I give (Philippians 4:17). First Corinthians 3:10-15 states that as I build on the foundation with gold, silver, and precious stones (people and God's work) versus wood, hay, and straw, it will not burn up and I will not suffer loss.

So when you and I give, we *do* get something in return. When we are rich toward God instead of rich toward ourselves, we get a solid foundation for the future—one that is not uncertain. When we believe we can't afford to give, that is a short-term focus that will ultimately result in loss. Everything here will be burned up, but what we send on ahead will be rewarded.

One more practical reason to give. Phil, like many others, missed the true cost of giving in the United States. In this country it doesn't always cost us a dollar to give a dollar. Because we can deduct some charitable giving dollars from our tax bill, our government helps fund some of our giving! If a person is in a 35 percent tax bracket, for example, for every dollar given the government funds 35 cents. So it only costs 65 cents to give a dollar!

Next Steps

Where are you on your giving journey? We've helped our clients give more than they ever thought possible by sharing these truths with them and helping them plan their finances. But not everyone walks through our doors ready to write big checks to their favorite charities. Giving more is a process.

I'm so thankful for Julie's influence early on in our marriage. She modeled and encouraged me to take some steps of faith in the area of giving. I'm grateful I realized I couldn't afford not to give. Not only have I had the joy of giving, it's encouraging to know I've been storing up a solid foundation for the future. I don't want to be like the rich man who ran out of life before he ran out of money (Luke 12). I want to be wise and not a fool. I want to be like the little boy in the following illustration of "two nickels and five pennies":

> When an ice cream sundae cost much less than it does today, a boy entered a coffee shop and sat at a table. A waitress put a glass of water in front of him.
>
> "How much is an ice cream sundae?" he asked.
>
> "Fifty cents," replied the waitress.
>
> The little boy pulled his hand out of his pocket and studied a number of coins in it.
>
> "How much is a dish of plain ice cream?" he inquired.
>
> Some people were now waiting for a table, and the waitress was becoming impatient. "Thirty-five cents," she said hurriedly.
>
> The little boy again counted the coins. "I'll have the plain ice cream."
>
> The waitress brought the ice cream and walked away.

The boy finished, paid the cashier, and departed. When the waitress returned to his vacated table, she found two nickels and five pennies placed neatly beside his empty dish.

The boy could have indulged in the sundae, but instead he got plain ice cream so he could be generous with the waitress. A huge tip! We can take a lesson and strive to be generous like this little boy.

❊ THINKING IT THROUGH ❊

❏ Do you find yourself thinking like Phil?

❏ Do you consider yourself generous?

❏ What kind of foundation are you storing up?

❏ Do you believe you can give and still accomplish your other objectives?

❏ Can you think of a time in your life when you stretched in your giving? How did it feel?

11

INVEST IN THIS

Jana Hunt was a woman on a mission. The brilliant 30-year-old knew what she wanted out of life. She would land a partnership in a prestigious law firm, make some sound investments, get married, and retire at 40. Jana was focused. Extremely popular growing up, she now kept her social life to a minimum. She considered dating a distraction.

After graduating from North Carolina State, Jana tackled Duke's Law and Entrepreneurship LLM program. By finishing third in her class, she attracted interest from a Charlotte law firm that was searching for a woman with Jana's skill set. When the partners met Jana, they hired her immediately. Goal number one was well underway.

Looking around her new office, Jana's eyes came to rest on the neatly framed picture of her parents on the corner of her desk. She remembered how her mother had always put the needs of others ahead of her own. She had even put her travel dreams on hold after she met her future husband at college. Those dreams were never realized because her mom's life was cut short by cancer when Jana was only 15.

Jana's dad was a devoted worker for Child Protective Services. His fulfilling position didn't pay very well, so the family struggled to make ends meet. Although her dad never complained, Jana vowed she'd never be dependent on someone to take care of her again. That's what investments were for, she decided.

Her drive to succeed, along with her expert planning skills, kept Jana in perpetual motion. She rarely took a day off and seldom stopped to pause, read, or reflect. She had no desire for another perspective; she liked the one she had. But when life deals a hard enough blow, even the most driven are forced to slow down.

Shortly after she was hired in Charlotte, her father suffered a severe stroke. He lingered for months before passing. Today Jana was driving to Raleigh to meet with Charley Harris, her dad's long-time friend, financial advisor, and the executor of her dad's will.

"Hello, Jana," Charley said as the young woman entered his office. "Please have a seat. May I get you anything to drink?"

"Thank you, Mr. Harris. I'm fine right now," Jana said as she took the offered seat.

"Well, tell me how you're doing, and tell me about Charlotte. Are you keeping all of those old codgers in line over there?" Charley teased.

"It's been great," Jana said. "The partners have been very gracious throughout Dad's illness. They've been like family. I told them we were meeting today, and they encouraged me to take the entire day off. Which reminds me, I never did get to thank you for your referral letter. It made quite an impression on Mr. Pierce and his sons."

"I've known Bob since law school, and he's a good man," Charley said with a slight grin. "He's had a handful with those boys though. I hope you're not letting those high rollers push you around!"

"No, sir. But thanks again for the recommendation. I know it helped."

"I'm sure you didn't need my letter to win them over," Charley replied as he fidgeted in his seat. "They were sold on you the moment they met you. Now, are you sure I can't get you something to drink before we get started?"

Jana gave a reassuring smile. "I know this isn't easy, Mr. Harris. But you can relax. I know the protocol. I'm an attorney, remember?"

"Indeed you are, young lady," Charley responded as he reached for his water. "Let me just say one thing about your dad if I may."

"Certainly," Jana said.

"Your father was a special man, Jana," Charley said as tears formed in his eyes. "I don't think he ever really got over losing your mom. He went to work every day with a heavy heart. And the issues he had to deal with in Child Services—I don't know how he did it, to tell you the truth."

"He said he did it by the grace of God," Jana replied.

"That's right," Charley agreed. "You dad was a strong believer."

"But *why* did he do it? That's the question I can't answer," Jana added. "All those stressful years at what was basically a dead-end job."

"You don't know why?" Charley asked, looking at her quizzically.

"Well, it sure wasn't for the money," Jana said.

"That's certainly true!"

"Then *why*? Dad was sharp. He could have worked in a lot of places. But I watched him give his life to a system that totally abused him. And what's worse—he did it for peanuts!"

"Jana, your dad didn't give his life to a system. He invested his life in people."

Jana paused. "You're right, Mr. Harris. Mom and I did without while Dad invested in other people who couldn't care less about us."

"Did you ever tell your father how you felt?" Charley asked.

"I tried to!" Jana exclaimed. "But all he'd say was, 'Honey, I think I'm really making a difference in the lives of kids who don't have a dad.'"

"Wasn't that true?" Charley asked.

Jana hesitated. "Mr. Harris, do you know how many times Dad came home late because Child Services couldn't decide what to do with a kid? Do you know how many times my dad brought a child home because there was no other place for him or her to go? I watched the system take my father from me while I sat at home wishing I had one. And what did he get? He earned peanuts and lived just long enough to watch his 401(k) go in the tank. What's the ROI—the 'return on investment'—on that?"

"Jana, I'm sure your dad told you that some investments just can't be measured that way."

"A hundred times," Jana responded, looking away.

Charley could see that Jana felt slighted by her dad's choices. He gave her a moment before he continued. "Jana, what did you think about your dad's funeral service?"

"Well, it reflected my father, that's for sure. Why do you ask, Mr. Harris?"

"Well, what did you think about the testimonies from those four young men? Did they give you a little more insight into what your dad's life was all about? You know, if time had allowed, there could have been 20 young men up there giving tribute to your dad."

"I'm not here to change what my dad did, Mr. Harris. I just know that I'm not giving my life to people or a system that doesn't care about me," Jana said confidently. "Now, about my dad's estate..."

Charley opened a folder and walked through the details of Jana's father's estate.

As Jana expected, her dad was a simple man. He'd been a steady plodder all of his life, and his investments showed it. Even though their home was small, it was paid for. But his county retirement fund was larger than she'd expected.

When they finished with the details, Charley said, "Those were your dad's *working* assets. Two other things will bring closure to your dad's estate. Major medical covered all of his hospital costs, but didn't cover a large portion of the special care needed in the nursing home. That's the bad news. The good news is that your dad maintained a very nice term-life policy that covers all of those needs. After taxes and expenses, this should leave you with about $200,000 and the house, which you can rent for income or sell."

Jana sat stunned for a few moments. "Are you sure about that amount, Mr. Harris?"

"Yes," Charley answered. "It'll take about two weeks to settle everything, and then we'll get a check for you. It's not a fortune, I know, but it's what your dad had."

"I'm surprised," Jana said. "I didn't know if there was going to be anything left after the nursing home expenses. I would have been happy just breaking even."

"Well, I know he wanted you to have as much as possible, so he planned accordingly. I trust you'll make some wise investments with the money, just like your dad did."

"Don't worry about that, Mr. Harris," Jana assured him. "Do you realize what this does for me?"

"It helps you pay off your student loans?" Charley offered. "Your dad was a little worried about that, you know."

"Oh, Dad did hate the student loan thing. The loan is $80,000 with interest at 7 percent. I think I may be able to earn significantly more than that by investing the money. A couple of people in the firm are doing great with gas and coffee futures right now. I just haven't had any money to get in on that. But now I do!"

"I'd be very careful, Jana," Charley cautioned. "Futures are a very high risk."

"I know, but the reward is so worth it. Skip, Mr. Pierce's oldest son, made $50,000 in two months. That could lead to an early retirement—and that's one of my goals."

"You know, we always hear about what someone made in futures. Next time you're with Bob Pierce, ask him if anyone in the firm has ever *lost* money in futures."

"I couldn't pry into someone's finances like that, Mr. Harris. But futures aren't the only investments out there. Our firm also represents some venture capitalists who are making a fortune right now funding business intelligence software development."

"Explain that to me, Jana," Charley asked.

"Explain what?" Jana asked.

"Tell me about how your investment will be used specifically in development of 'BI' software. Do you understand how it works? I sure don't."

"Well, it's pretty complicated," Jana acknowledged. "It's sort of a black box and hard to explain, but I know the guys who invested a few years ago made a bundle. My understanding is this investment returns close to 20 percent even in down markets."

"Jana, you're a very bright young lady with a terrific future ahead of you. Be careful about investing in anything you can't explain or with people you don't really know," Charley cautioned.

"I appreciate your concern, Mr. Harris, but you can rest easy. The guys in our firm never invest in anything that doesn't guarantee a good return. We're attorneys, remember!" Jana said with a smile.

Charley stood up and returned her smile. "Jana, before you leave, I'd like to ask one favor of you."

"Sure, Mr. Harris. You've done a lot for me. What can I do for you?" Jana asked sincerely.

"Here's my card. Promise me that before you make any investments, you'll call me and tell me about them. Then we'll take that investment before the Lord in prayer."

"You want me to *pray* with you before I invest any money?" Jana asked.

"That's all I'm asking," Charley said. "Tell me about it, and we'll pray about it."

"I guess I can do that," Jana agreed.

Jana was overwhelmed as she began her three-hour drive home. She knew her dad loved her, but she'd never once dreamed he'd leave her enough money to invest for the future. This would be a huge boost toward her goal of early retirement. She was just about to turn the radio up and celebrate when her cell phone rang. Seeing the word "office" on the screen, she turned the radio off.

"Hello!" Jana answered.

"Jana, Skip Pierce here. How are you?"

"I'm fine, Mr. Pierce. And how are you?"

"I'm doing well too. Dad said you had an important meeting today, and I wanted to see if it went okay. I know life has been tough for you lately."

"That's very kind of you. Yes, everything is fine. Actually it's great!" Jana said.

"Terrific!" Skip responded. "Glad to hear that. Hey, listen, I know it's short notice, but a few of us are meeting for steaks at Spencer's tonight. I thought you'd like to join us."

"Spencer's on the River!" Jana exclaimed. "Wow, that's high cotton!"

"It's not our nickel, either!" Skip said. "This is on the VC Group we represent. They're in town from Boston, and I want you to meet them. Can you make it by six o'clock?"

"Absolutely!" Jana replied. "I'll be there."

Jana clutched her phone in disbelief and reveled in what had just happened. Skip Pierce was calling her! He was inviting her to dine with the people she'd been dying to meet. What a turnaround this was. This morning she was dreading this day, but now she had a windfall inheritance and connections with the "big boys." Goal number two was closer than she'd thought.

As Jana placed her phone on the console, she felt something at the tip of her fingers. It was Charley's card, which she'd placed there when she'd gotten into the car. This time she noticed his tag line: *Investing in what really matters.*

Jana felt her heart sink. This might be one promise she just couldn't keep...

⚭

> **The Lie:** "I can get rich quick."
>
> **The Truth:** "He who tills his land will have plenty of food, but he who follows empty pursuits will have poverty in plenty. A faithful man will abound with blessings, but he who makes haste to be rich will not go unpunished" (Proverbs 28:19-20).
> "Those who want to get rich fall into temptation and a snare and many foolish and harmful desires which plunge men into ruin and destruction" (1 Timothy 6:9).

What will happen next for Jana? What will she do with her newfound money? Will she call Charley as she promised? Will she pay off student loans or invest her windfall in futures? Will she try to get rich quick so she can reach her goal of retiring at age 40? Losing both parents while still young was rough, but career-wise, her trajectory couldn't be better. Her investment decisions today will make a huge impact on her future financial condition.

We've talked a lot in this book about gaining God's perspective on financial decisions. The houses we buy, the vocations we choose, and the cars we own are all building blocks for our financial future. So what is God's perspective on investments? Let's look briefly at the role of investments in our financial lives and then the process for investing.

Role of Investments

I tell my clients very clearly that people gain wealth by spending less than they make over a long period of time and *preserving capital* with their investments. We do not accumulate wealth through investments only. As a matter of fact, I don't know of any one of our more than 5000 clients who have made his or her wealth through investments only. Candidly, most people don't believe this truth.

> If we remember that the role of investments
> is to *preserve* wealth, not *create* wealth,
> we will make better financial decisions.

When it comes to investments, I find that the majority of people have a *Money Magazine* mentality. Cover stories tout the highest return mutual funds or the latest real estate techniques for getting rich quick. The articles show how success happened for this family or individual and how it can be around the corner for every reader. Headlines sell magazines, but I have yet to meet someone who read a magazine and became financially independent because of it.

I've found that if we remember that the role of investments is to *preserve* wealth, not *create* wealth, we will make better financial decisions. We will be less apt to succumb to the lie that we can "get rich quick."

The Process of Investing

To make sound investment decisions, first we need to make sure we have money to invest. This means that after living expenses, taxes, giving, and debt payments, we have a positive margin. If we do, then we have money to invest. Or, as in Jana's case, we may have inheritances or other pools of capital available.

How do we prudently invest a positive margin or surplus cash? One thing for sure, it's not by looking at the opportunities we hear about around the water cooler, over lunch, or at church. Those conversations are anecdotes at best, and they rarely contain all the facts necessary to paint an accurate picture of the investment.

We advise clients to use our Sequential Investment Strategy for making investment decisions. The diagram on the next page illustrates this process. I've found that if we follow these steps, we won't live the investment lie. We will, instead, build a solid financial foundation.

SEQUENTIAL INVESTMENT STRATEGY

Long-term Goals—Growth
5 years plus

4

Short-term Goals—Liquidity
6 months to 5 years

3

2

1

Eliminate all high-interest/ short-term debt	Keep 6 to 12 months' living expenses in a Money Market Fund (MMF) or savings account	Save for major purchases using a MMF, CD, or treasury bills (potentially a mutual fund)	Diversify to meet long-term goals investing in: MMF/CDs/ Treasuries Mutual Funds Real Estate Bonds Equities
Credit cards Automobiles Small debt	Reserves to protect in case of disability, accidents, or any emergency	Automobiles Furniture Down payment on a house	Retirement College for children Financial freedom Vacation home Travel Pay off mortgage Develop own business

The first step calls for paying off short-term debt. I still find it amazing that people don't understand that paying off a credit card debt, vehicle loan, or student loan is a guaranteed way to earn whatever interest rate is being charged on the debt. For example, paying off a credit card with a 12 percent interest rate is the equivalent of earning that same 12 percent in an investment. The big difference is that paying off the 12 percent credit card is like getting a *risk-free rate of return of 12 percent*. Often people have some personal debt, some cash in the bank, and sometimes some mutual funds. When they ask us where to invest, we tell them they can get the best return by *paying off high-interest debt*, such as credit cards. Investments have risk; paying off debt does not.

I often get asked, "What about taxes?" Typically most investment returns are given in "before tax" terms. Therefore, it's consistent to compare the interest rate on any debt being paid off with the investment return as just stated.

Step two requires setting aside cash for emergencies. We recommend setting aside 6 to 12 months of living expenses in an emergency fund. This isn't the advice clients are usually looking for. After all, when our friends are sharing about their venture capital funds, sharing about our cash invested in a money market fund earning low interest isn't very exciting.

So why does this make sense? Why is it so prudent? Let's look at a not-too-improbable scenario using Jana as our illustration. Let's say that Jana, as the most recent hire at the firm, gets laid off in a recession. No other job is in sight. Her $2000 monthly mortgage and $500 student loan payments continue, her BMW drops a $4500 transmission, her dog just needed $1500 of vet care, and her washer and dryer need to be replaced. Jana (who skipped saving for emergencies) tries to get her money out of the venture capital fund (which is step four), but it has a five-year lockup term. And banks won't lend to someone unemployed. What can she do?

Jana would do what most people with no liquidity do—turn to her credit cards to get by. She will charge most purchases and take advantage of those cash advance offers she gets in the mail, meaning she could be charged a whopping interest rate of 24 percent! Even if the venture capital investment returns are high, it's doubtful it will earn a 24 percent compounded return. At this point, Jana will wish she had taken Charley up on his offer to pray about and discuss investment decisions. That dull money market fund containing cash for emergences would look pretty good to her now.

The third step is to save for major purchases. I have found that this is often the most difficult. Depending on your living expenses, hopefully you have $10,000 to $40,000 set aside for emergencies (Step 2). This third step requires even more funds to be set aside in an unexciting, low-earning liquid investment, such as a CD or money market fund. A 20 percent down payment on a house could be $20,000 to $40,000. Then there's saving another $15,000 to $25,000 for the next vehicle. And don't forget several thousand for furniture.

These expenses could require an additional $40,000 to $75,000 saved in a low-interest account. This number typically shocks people! After all, they want to get to investing in something exciting that has the potential to make their money grow faster. That's where the action is—not having thousands sitting in a dull, low-interest CD. But skipping this step can be disastrous to a person's long-term financial health!

Remember the true role of investments. *They are to preserve capital.* If you skip saving for major purchases, just like in our job-loss scenario, you could end up financing a car at 10 percent or paying mortgage insurance because you can't make a 20 percent down payment on a house, all while taking risks with the investments you do have to try to make up for it.

I know we don't earn much on these "cash" investments, but it's what you're avoiding paying in interest that's the real earnings. Avoiding car notes, mortgage insurance, and other interest charges adds up quickly. Julie and I have followed this process, and we're grateful we did. We are proof that it can be done. Remember, plodding along brings prosperity.

Step four is where we begin investing. There are three keys for any investments. Here are the first two:

- Only invest funds you can leave in the investment for *a long time*. This allows you to weather the inevitable ups and downs of any investment market.

- *Diversify* your investments. "Cast your bread on the surface of the waters, for you will find it after many days. Divide your portion to seven, or even to eight, for you do not know what misfortune may occur on the earth" (Ecclesiastes 11:1-2).

I know many real estate investors who ignored the principle of diversification. They believed that investing in real estate was the only way to make significant money. Many of them, all experts in their real estate niche, kept rolling their profits from one deal to more and bigger deals, while increasing their leverage (debt balances). They never took any of their profits and placed them into other asset classes, such as stocks and bonds and cash. They also typically were loath to pay off debt because of the profits available with leverage. When the real estate crash occurred, many lost their properties, their business, and in some cases their personal possessions to satisfy their bank debts. If only they had diversified into other asset classes! They would have been much better off. This also occurred with many people who didn't diversify during the technology stock boom. When that bubble burst, they too were probably wishing they had applied this principle.

And here's the third investment key:

- Remember *risk and reward* go together. Many investments earn a higher return over the long run, but not at the rates Jana was hearing from her friends. And few investments are *guaranteed*. Charley Harris was right. People freely talk about the good investments they've made and rarely share about the ones that went into the dumpster. Investments that earn 50 percent in two months have high risk or are potentially fraudulent. Countless "Ponzi schemes" promising high returns have duped many. *No investment return is guaranteed.* The word "guaranteed" should *never* be attached to an investment return because it is just not true.

"I want to get a high return with no risk" is a mantra I hear often. That is impossible. Why? Because risk and reward are inextricably linked. I show clients how the different categories of investments have performed during different economic periods to give them realistic expectations for returns on their funds.

> Wealth is accumulated by spending less than
> we make and is preserved with investments.

Stop and think about it. If risk wasn't related to reward, everybody would be wealthy by making high-return investments. Saving any amount in low-interest money market funds or following the Sequential Investment Strategy wouldn't make sense. But because high returns are related to risk, it is wise to follow the strategies I've outlined. It's likely that you or someone you know has lost money in an investment. You know this risk/return principle is true, but it's easy to lose track of it in the excitement of an investing opportunity.

Before leaving this issue of risk, I frequently ask this question to determine a person's risk tolerance: "Would you be more upset if you didn't make the investment and it went up 50 percent or if you did make it and it went down 50 percent?" Most people prefer to *avoid the loss,* which tells me they're more conservative than they think they are.

Another good caveat on investments: *If you don't understand the investment completely or can't explain it so your spouse or someone else can understand it, don't invest in it.* This discipline can steer us away from most bad investments. Bernie Madoff, the perpetuator of one of the largest Ponzi schemes in history, lost more than $50 billion dollars for his investors. Madoff promised a guaranteed return of no less than 12 percent per year, and the money flowed in from investors. When due diligence professionals and potential investors asked for details on his trading strategies, he refused to give them specifics. That should have scared off many investors, but it didn't. The allure of a steady, above-market, relatively risk-free return caused people to set aside common sense.

So what about Jana? With her father's inheritance, she has some decisions to make. She is at a crossroads. Her financial foundation will depend on the direction she chooses. She has two very different options.

Option 1: She can invest her $200,000 in an attempt to get the maximum rate of return to support her goal of retiring in ten years. This means she...

- would not pay off any of her school debt
- would not set aside any funds for inevitable emergencies
- would be investing part of her funds in something she can't fully explain, such as coffee futures
- would be investing the rest in a risky venture capital fund seeking the highest return possible
- would sell the house and invest that money in another risky market, such as gas futures

Option 2: Jana could apply the Sequential Investing Strategy and extend her time horizon for retirement past 40, giving her investments more time to grow and enabling her to reach her objectives with less risky investments that may have a lower but steadier growth rate. She would...

- pay off her school loans (thus saving 7 percent interest)
- set aside $30,000 for an emergency fund (avoiding future credit card and loan interest payments)
- invest her remaining $90,000 in a diversified portfolio of mutual funds
- keep the house as a diversifier to the mutual funds. This would be a real asset-producing income with some tax benefits.

There are a lot of important truths shared in this book, but this one has the potential to give you the most peace of mind. Once I understood that wealth is accumulated by spending less than I make and is preserved with investments, I didn't buy the lie that I could get rich through my investments. I hope Jana understands that as well and knows she needs to focus on her passion and calling of being a great attorney. Her focus shouldn't be on getting rich quick.

I hope she takes Charley's suggestion and calls him before making investments. I also hope she will focus on investments that really matter: *people*. I want her to seek to be rich like her father—rich in relationships. After all, in the scope of eternity investing in people is what really matters.

◈ THINKING IT THROUGH ◈

❏ Have you ever made a bad financial investment? What did you learn?

❏ Explain a time when you experienced the risk and reward principle.

❏ What might keep you from starting the Sequential Investment Strategy today?

❏ What can you do to invest in people?

❏ Do you have peace of mind regarding your financial investments?

12

FLORIDA OR BUST!

"Doris, please hurry up! If we don't hit the road now, we won't make it in time." Fred was getting anxious. His goal was to be in central Florida by nightfall. He and his wife, Doris, had waited for this day almost their entire lives.

"I'm almost ready, honey! Be right there!" Doris hollered back as she stuffed one more item into her second suitcase. Fred had always been a little pushy, and she was used to that. But she thought today would be different. After all, didn't they have the rest of their lives in front of them?

As the trunk shut tight on their big, blue Buick, Fred looked at his wife of 43 years. Doris had worked as hard as he had, and the two of them could hardly contain themselves. They were heading south to pick out the perfect spot to retire. As soon as their present house sold, they'd be in Florida for good. No more shoveling snow and no more punching the time clock.

Doris was 64 and had worked in the school system in Dalton County for more than 30 years. Fred had just turned 66 and had been with the same manufacturing company for almost 40 years.

Just two days prior, both had put in their last day of work. As they pulled out of the city limits of Cleveland, Ohio, that morning, they couldn't help but reminisce.

"Honey, I can't believe we're finally doing this!" Doris exclaimed. "I thought we'd never reach this point in our lives. Think about it, Fred. You and me *retired*!"

"Yeah, I hear you!" echoed Fred. "In one way I hate to leave something I put so much time into. But I don't think I could have worked another year under Benson. That CEO is one tough cookie. Worst thing about him is he's a food industry guy. He's clueless about manufacturing. How does the Board of Directors find these people? You'd think they'd want to hire from within."

"You've been saying that for years, Fred. But just think, you no longer have to worry about it. That's somebody else's problem. You're retired now!" Doris said with an encouraging grin. "You're retired and you deserve it."

"You got that right!" Fred agreed. "I *do* deserve it. Heck, we both do. We paid a big price to get to this point."

"That's for sure," concurred Doris. "Remember all those years we had to choose between family vacations or funding our retirement plans to the max? Missing vacations seemed hard at the time, but looking at our retirement statements now, it was worth it. Besides, we have all the time in the world to see the kids now. It's all working out!"

"I just hope they have time for us," Fred sighed. "You know how busy our kids are, and those grandkids keep them hopping."

"We've lived in that world," Doris mused. "Running all over the place for recitals, school events, ball games, and the like. When you're in the middle of it, you think it'll never end."

"Yep, we were always running to something, weren't we? Don't get me wrong, I don't have many regrets," Fred said. "But I do wish we'd had more time for the weekend stuff."

"Like what?" Doris asked.

"You know, the stuff that only happens on weekends, such as camping trips and coaching Little League. You can't commit to those things and still be available to grab those overtime days. I knew if we wanted to retire in good shape, I'd have to keep my nose down. I'm sure the kids understood."

"I'm sure they do now, honey. Providing the immediate needs of our family and providing for retirement wasn't easy, but you did great!" Doris affirmed with a squeeze of Fred's arm. "And if it's any consolation, I feel the same way. We just couldn't do everything."

Fred continued to think about that exchange when a Cracker Barrel sign caught his eye. "How about some lunch?" Fred blurted as he slowed for the exit ramp.

"Sounds great!" Doris said. "I am a little hungry, and I need to stretch my legs." The thoughts about the kids and how fast time had gone had caused her to pause. She found herself silently hoping that retirement really would be what they'd dreamed.

An hour later, as the couple left the restaurant, Fred rubbed his stomach, which was considerably larger than it was 40 years ago. "Wow, what a meal!"

Forty years ago, not only was Fred's stomach in better shape, so was the rest of him. Back then he had excelled on the church softball and basketball teams. But between working long hours and raising kids, Fred had gradually let himself go. One of the joys he was looking forward to was all of the retirement community amenities. Most had basketball courts, ball fields, and really nice golf courses. He would finally have the time to take care of himself.

Seeing that lunch had made Doris sleepy, Fred suggested she take a little nap. As Doris slept, Fred thought about how quickly the years had gone by. It seemed like just yesterday he stood on the stage and held up his degree. Fortunate to land a job with Gerard and Company, he'd enjoyed his work and advanced through the ranks. Fred always made a good income, along with nice bonuses most years. But still things seemed to always be tight. There was never enough to pay down his 30-year mortgage early. It took 15 years to pay off the student loans for college, but there wasn't much else he could have done. It still frustrated him that there never had seemed to be enough time left over for the vacations he wanted to take with the kids.

Fred knew that part of the reason it had been so tight all those years was because he had been committed to maximizing the funding of his retirement plan through the company. Early on it was a defined contribution plan. Over the past ten years it had been a 401(k). It seemed like a no-lose deal to fund it to the max since the company offered a generous matching program. He and his buddies agreed that it would be silly to leave that on the table. As he reflected on that decision and recalled the combined total he had amassed in the two plans, a slight grin creased his face. That's what made this day possible. Doris had done the same with her retirement, so now they were sitting pretty.

"What are you grinning about?" asked Doris, opening her eyes from her nap.

"Just reflecting on how much we have in our retirement accounts," Fred said with a smile.

"I hope it's enough to move into the East Cotton States Community!" Doris said. "Don't we meet Bob there tomorrow to look around?"

"Yes, we meet him at eight in the morning," Fred answered. "He has several places to show us. It should be fun."

The next morning at eight, Fred and Doris were right on time to meet Bob.

"Good morning, Bob," Fred said with enthusiasm as he stretched out his hand. "What do you have to show us today?"

"Well, guys, I think today is going to be your lucky day," beamed

Bob. "We have several of our newer places available both on the golf course and with a lake view, and they're all a short walk to the clubhouse. One of them should be perfect for you!"

"Oh boy!" exclaimed Doris. "I can hardly wait."

Over the next few days Bob, Fred, and Doris studied dozens of options. Finally, they settled on a spacious ranch home overlooking the lake and not far from the clubhouse. It was the perfect location, and it made the ultimate statement about their new situation in life. When Fred and Doris signed the purchase agreement, they felt like the brass ring they'd coveted all of these years was clearly in sight.

Six months later Fred and Doris still couldn't believe it. Their home in Cleveland had sold in less than three weeks, and now they were settled in at East Cotton States. Many in the community were from the Midwest, so it was easy for them to make new friends. Before they knew it, they were involved in shuffleboard tournaments, a bridge club, and bocce ball games. Fred even managed an occasional round of golf. Besides that, they loved the free time.

Though he walked past them every day, Fred couldn't take advantage of the basketball courts or softball fields. Years ago he had tweaked his shoulder at a "meet and greet" golf outing, and he had never had the time for the procedure the doctor recommended. Fred's health wasn't as good as he'd thought. His additional weight had taken a toll on his knees, and his blood pressure was on the rise. The doctors discouraged him from jogging, and his five prescription medicines made him feel a little lethargic.

Doris was in very good health, but the abundance of free time was more than she had bargained for. After three book-group meetings, scrapbooking with her new Midwest friends, and heading up a butterfly garden beautification project, Doris found herself inexplicably longing for her old routine. Yet it pained her to think that her old routine had for so many years caused her to miss some special times with each of the kids. Now she found herself spending more and more hours on the back porch, leafing through family pictures and looking at the lake.

In truth, Doris missed the kids more than she told Fred. She'd called both of them and had given them open invitations. She couldn't wait to show them their new place. They promised to come as soon as they could, but right now it was impossible for them to commit. And when she offered to come their way, it seemed like an effort for them to work a visit from them in. This wasn't shaping up into the dream retirement she'd pictured.

Well into their new life, Fred suggested they start having dinner out on the back porch. He wanted to eat while overlooking the lake. After all, they'd spent the extra $10,000 to have the best view, and it would be silly to not enjoy it more often. Doris didn't say a word, but the idea didn't sit well with her. In her mind, she'd already spent way too much time in that very spot thinking about those she missed most. Often her back-porch sessions ended in her losing the battle to fight back tears.

Evenings were quiet at East Cotton States. The only sounds heard after five o'clock were residents in golf carts headed to the club or the huge fountain spraying in the lake. After another dinner with little conversation, the two of them sat and stared over the calm water. After a while, Doris spoke up with a question she'd been pondering for more than two months.

"Fred, I have a question," Doris began as she looked down and reached for her husband's hand.

"What is it?" Fred asked as he reached for hers.

"Well, it's about time," Doris said, looking back over the lake.

"About time for dessert?" Fred asked, trying to make Doris smile.

"No, I'm serious, Fred." Doris went on. "I have a question about our time, and I want to know if you have the same question."

"Okay, ask away," Fred said.

"Well, we just spent 40 years getting ready to come here, right?"

"Is that your question? How many years it took us to get here?" Fred asked with surprise. "Come on, Doris, you know the answer to that."

"Yes, I do. Now here's my question: How come those 40 years went by in a flash, but each day here seems to drag on forever?"

Fred didn't say a word. He merely looked at the lake.

"And while we're at it, honey," Doris continued, "how come when we were busy, we missed doing the things that really mattered, but now that we've got all the time in the world, nothing we do seems to matter at all?"

After a while, Fred managed to look at his wife calmly. He knew what she said was true. He'd had the same thoughts. But how does a husband tell his wife that what they'd worked for all of their lives didn't seem to be working out at all?

⚜

THE LIE: "Retirement is the ultimate goal of working hard."

Unfortunately, Doris and Fred aren't alone. Millions of us have bought this lie. We work (or overwork) so we can quit and enjoy life. Isn't that what all the commercials tell us? In addition to paying the bills, funding education, paying down debt, we also have the stress of squeezing out the funds to maximize our pension plans so we can quit working as early as possible.

In reality, retirement is a twentieth-century phenomenon that has added stress to our lives. And it starts early. My college-age son called one day and said, "Hey, Dad, my teacher said I should fund a Roth IRA. What do you think about that?"

So how should we look at retirement? What *is* retirement? Where did the idea originate? What, if anything, should we be doing about it?

The word "retirement" is not
mentioned in the Bible.

What Is Retirement?

The word "retirement" is not mentioned in the Bible. We find the word "retire" a few times, but it's related to withdrawing from battle for a period of time. We never see it used in the way we use it today—as quitting one's vocation (work) for a life of leisure.

With this modern definition, we immediately are confronted with the truths that counteract this lie:

> THE TRUTH: We are COMMANDED to work
> (1 Thessalonians 4:11), work is a GIFT (Ecclesiastes 5:18-19), and it is GOOD (Genesis 2:15).
> "If anyone will not work, neither let him eat" (2 Thessalonians 3:10 AMP).

We will unpack these truths in more detail in chapter 15, but suffice it to say that if work is good for us and commanded by God, a goal to *not* work and live a life of leisure may leave us unfulfilled and empty. There's nothing wrong with quitting what we're currently doing as long as we continue to work or contribute to our families or society in some capacity. To do *nothing* productive is not good.

The Concept of Retirement

So where did we get the idea of retirement, and how did it

become so ingrained into our consciousness? Let's look at a time line of retirement in the United States: [1]

Pre-industrial: This is defined as primarily the time before the Civil War, when society was largely agrarian. Retirement did not exist during this time. There was never the idea of sidelining (retiring) older workers. They stayed involved until late in life for their wisdom, insights, and judgment.

Post Civil War: America began to move toward being more industrialized. More focus on companies, corporations, factories, more urban and less agrarian. This change laid the groundwork for the concept of retirement to take root.

Early 1900s: As American industry continued to expand into the twentieth century, older individuals began to be looked at as more of a drain on society than as useful, contributing members of society. "Old" in the early 1900s was someone in his or her forties, if you can believe it! Anyone over 60 was considered unproductive.

1933: At the bottom of the Great Depression with more than 13 million young men out of work, President Franklin D. Roosevelt succumbed to pressure to install public pensions to encourage older men to retire and get younger men working. This led to the enactment of the Social Security Act of 1935, the launching pad of retirement as we know it today.

To pay for this pension plan, the Act called for current workers to be taxed to provide for those who retired. The age to receive benefits was 65 (still many people's mental retirement target); at that time life expectancy was 63. What has been lost over time is that when Social Security was enacted, a person was not expected to live and draw benefits as long as we do now, and the payout was only intended to provide a subsistence lifestyle. It was during this time that the image of an old widow eating cat food in a dimly lit apartment emerged. Not what Fred and Doris worked so hard for, was it? So what happened?

1940s: The unions bargained for private pensions in companies versus pay raises. The tax laws allowed deductions, but the future retirement obligation didn't show up on a company's books. During this time pensions became more and more mainstream.

1950s: Business, labor, government, and most of the insurance and financial industries promoted retirement aggressively. Newsletters and magazines began to carry stories of happily retired people, along with pictures of them playing golf in the mountains or enjoying leisure on the beach. Retirement was implanted in the minds of all Americans as the ultimate goal. A leisurely old age was the reward for all the hard work. Retirement painted an idyllic lifestyle for everyone.

It never ceases to amaze me that the commercials promoting retirement today hold to what began in the 1950s. They use phrases like, "Enjoy the life you were meant for" or "Really live life." I always smile and think, "Why not enjoy life now? Why wait? Do I really want to put all my focus on enjoying life when I'm 65?"

All too often, as Fred and Doris found out, by the time people get to retirement, their health is typically on the decline and most of the things they wanted to do they can no longer do. The root and insidiousness of this money lie may be that it makes it harder to live in balance today.

In addition, retirement has turned out to be not so golden for many people:

> According to a poll cited by American Demographics, 41% of retirees say it was a difficult adjustment. This is an astronomical figure considering that only 12% saw marriage as a difficult adjustment and 23% thought becoming parents was difficult.[2]

> The story of how Lee Iacocca [famous Chrysler CEO] in his own words "flunked retirement" is a cautionary tale for anyone who holds a job, from CEO on down. After you unwrap yourself from work, it's easy to find yourself at loose ends. Figuring out what to do next can be particularly difficult.[3]

What Should We Do About Retirement?

Make retirement part of the plan—not THE plan. First, I'm not totally anti-retirement. If someone has plenty of margin and can easily afford to fund a retirement plan at work and take advantage of the favorable tax deferral, that's a good planning option. Many people in the public sector also have retirement income provided for them. However, it's my observation that if retirement is someone's sole focus, there is typically imbalance in the other components of a sound financial plan. The result is lack of financial freedom. Prudent steps such as establishing an emergency fund or paying off debt are overlooked.

Make retirement part of the
plan—not THE plan.

I can't tell you how many folks I've met with who had $100,000 in their 401(k) and $100,000 in credit card debt. They were borrowing to fund their retirement by overspending—and they didn't even realize it. Or they were classic examples of having a lot of money in a retirement account and very little in an emergency fund. A retirement plan is of little use when the septic tank goes out, the car breaks down, or they have an unexpected medical bill.

I recommend that you make sure you're not using credit card debt and that you have 6 to 12 months in living expenses set aside in an emergency fund before fully funding your retirement plan each year. You should also save for major purchases: cars, education costs, home remodeling, and so on. What you put in retirement savings should be part of an overall plan—not the most important part of the plan with first call on your funds.

> To accumulate cash or pay off debt, you may
> have to cut back on your retirement funding.

I know what the world teaches: If your company offers a great deal and matches your retirement contribution, go all out. But no matter how great a deal it is, when you have to use your credit cards for emergencies, you immediately mitigate how "great" the retirement plan actually is.

When I speak on this topic of retirement, I'm often asked if money should be taken out of a retirement plan to establish an emergency fund or to pay off debt. In general, I don't recommend taking funds out of current retirement plans because of the penalties and taxes that have to be paid. I do, however, encourage a detailed review of personal cash flow. In many cases a reduction in the amount you're currently contributing into retirement is in order. To accumulate cash or pay off debt, you may have to cut back on your retirement funding amount. I know this contradicts the conventional wisdom of maximizing your company's match, but in many cases this will give you the balance and freedom in your cash flow that you need.

Julie and I have had several years in which we didn't fund our retirement plan at all. "Aren't you a financial advisor? Don't you understand compounding?" you ask. Yes and yes. But I've found that reestablishing an emergency fund (cash in the bank) or paying off debt on the house gave me more peace of mind. We have no regrets about that decision.

Extend your time horizon. I've found that by extending my retirement time horizon by even a few years, the pressure to accumulate retirement funds is reduced. Sixty-five is an outdated age to focus on retiring. When that age was set, life expectancy was 63. Today it's around 79 for men and women. With medical advances and the focus on health and fitness, our earning years have been expanded. By lengthening your time horizon and planning to work a few more years, you will reduce the amount you need to put away for retirement, which helps reduce current financial stress. As a matter of fact, if you plan to work your entire lifetime, you may experience more freedom and fulfillment. An article in *Worth* magazine some years ago noted: "No longer bound by the timetable that was arbitrarily set, you will be free to live longer, happier, healthier, and more rewarding lives. There will be no painful compromises to reach an artificial goal. There will be no finish line, no race."[4]

As we read the book of Acts, we find Paul living just like this. He hoped to finish his course and ministry (Acts 20:24) and continue to the end (2 Timothy 3:14). A proper understanding of retirement will allow us to more fully enjoy the trip! Going back to our story, I wonder if Fred and Doris regret not cutting back on retirement funding to spend a little more on family vacations.

Or perhaps they wish they'd worked less overtime to be able to coach or attend their children's athletic games and other activities. Sure they were able to put more in their retirement plans because they made more, but while they're gazing at the lake in East Cotton States, I wonder if they wish they'd balanced their lives more.

Stay productive. If you're planning to retire from your current vocation, plan now to focus on your next phase of life. There's nothing wrong with changing the form of your work. The problem is when you decide not to be productive at all. Endless rounds of golf or collecting seashells won't fulfill you. If you don't have a clear idea of a purposeful focus for your energy, then keep doing what you're doing. Don't retire for retirement's sake (this is what Fred and Doris did). Retire *to* something. As Lee Iacocca said, "The roof caves in on you because you haven't done enough thinking about who you are and what you should do with the rest of your life."[5] "Most peoples' self-esteem is maintained by being with a group of people who confirm and validate that what the person does is worthwhile," says Harvard psychologist Richard Geist. "Unfortunately for retirees, the people who provide that sense of validation all too often are one's co-workers."[6] Therefore, when we quit work, that validation source is removed and fulfillment is lacking. Business school professor Jeffrey Sonnenfeld called the jarring shift into retirement "a plunge into the abyss of insignificance."[7] This is what Doris and Fred began to feel after six months. Who are they now? What is their purpose?

In a *Fortune* magazine article, Betsy Morris wrote:

> The great baby boomer generation is facing later years
> that are likely to be more about job sharing than shuf-
> fleboard, more about shrinking entitlements than end-
> less journeys to romantic locales. Many silver-haired
> pioneers are living lives filled with work and real-world

achievement. They are experiencing the joys offered by
a busy, productive retirement.[8]

This article also reported on five couples and found that, for
them, retirement was about discovering what truly made them
happy as they aged together:

> For each the outcome was not what they once had
> hoped for. A woman who had longed to idle days away
> in London museums found fulfillment in the rough
> labors of farm work. A former English professor dis-
> covered he needed a platform for his views after all.
> A couple accustomed to the daily grind of building a
> business spend their days happily giving to others in a
> country far from home.[9]

You get the idea. It's fine to quit your vocation and retire, but
make sure you keep actively engaged in the world by working at
something, and that "something" needs to be purposeful.

Determine a purpose. The keys to life are to love and be loved, to
have some control over your environment, to successfully create
value in the world, and to have a meaningful purpose. Ephesians
5:15-17 tells us to "Live purposefully and worthily and accurately,
not as the unwise and witless, but as wise (sensible, intelligent
people), making the very most of the time (buying up each opportunity), because the days are evil. Therefore do not be vague and
thoughtless and foolish, but understanding what the will of the
Lord is" (AMP).

God wants us to have purpose around His Word and His
people—the only two things that last forever. The absence of this
purpose results in an emptiness in our lives. This focus on purpose
can be ignored to a large degree when busy working, but in retirement it's impossible to escape and can contribute to malaise and
lack of fulfillment.

Do not be in a hurry to quit.

Keep in mind that the retirement the World War II and Baby Boomer generation has enjoyed, or wants to enjoy, may be an extinct proposition. Listen to this: "The fact that that group has basically been able to take the last chapter of their lives off, paid, is a freak occurrence, a confluence of benefits that we're not likely to see again."[10] All the events that converged (Social Security, the post-World War II real estate boom, and aggressive defined benefit pensions) are all headed the opposite direction. But instead of being afraid you won't be able to retire, give thanks instead. "Retirement is a weird social experiment, a historical blip. Its collapse will be a triumph for common sense."[11]

So in summary, here's the deal. The goal of working is to fulfill God's mandate to be productive, to have our finances in order, and to lead purposeful lives with our family. It's not to retire (the lie). If in the process of working, people have extra margin (spending less than they make), saving for retirement is a good, tax-deferred choice. If there aren't extra funds, then people shouldn't feel like they're missing out by not funding retirement. If they accumulate sufficient funds to enable them to change the form of their productive work, great.

Do these ideas sound strange to you? My guess is they might. But ponder them. Accepting them might remove the pressure you feel to "hurry to quit" and allow you to achieve more balance in your life. How about it? Isn't it time to take back your life and live?

❧ THINKING IT THROUGH ❧

❏ What do you think about Russ's comments on retirement?

❏ Have you made retirement your primary focus?

❏ Do you think an "extended time horizon" will help you with balance?

❏ What would you do if you quit doing what you are doing now when you retire?

13

OUR BEST LAID PLANS

Les Shuler was a stickler for promptness. To him, being late was a sign of weakness and disorganization. Crossing the lobby of One Monarch Tower, Les glanced at his watch and picked up his pace. He wanted to be on the next elevator up.

"Seriously, Les! Do you really need to walk this fast?" his wife, Tiffany, complained as she tried to keep up. "These marble floors are as slick as glass!"

"I didn't tell you to wear four-inch spike heels," Les said without slowing down. "For a meeting you didn't want to go to, you sure managed to dress to the nines."

It was true. Tiffany wanted nothing to do with the upcoming meeting.

Arriving at the elevator doors, Les hit the arrow up button and checked his watch again.

Tiffany tapped Les's arm and pointed down the hall. "There's a Starbucks kiosk right over there. Let's grab a quick latte before we go up."

Les checked the elevator's progress before he spoke up.

"Holcomb and Dean bill at $400 an hour. Clock starts in about two minutes. Do the math, Tiffany. That 'quick latte' could cost about 60 bucks."

Reluctantly Tiffany followed Les into the elevator. He hit the button to the 25th floor.

As the elevator began its rapid rise, Tiffany could feel her palms getting damp.

This day was a long time in coming. After months of legal and marital wrangling, the trusts were in place and the wills were ready to be signed. Les and Tiffany had their family's future all planned out. Tiffany's only fear was whether they had done enough for the children.

Entering the office of Holcomb and Dean, a sharply dressed assistant greeted them. "Hello, Mr. and Mrs. Shuler. I'm Luke Stevens. I'll take your coats and get you situated in the north conference room. Mr. Dean will be joining you shortly."

"Thank you, Luke," Les acknowledged as he handed the young man their coats.

Luke motioned with his left hand. "Right this way, please." He escorted the couple down a hall and opened the door. "This room has the best view of the river," he pointed out. "May I get you something to drink?"

"Coffee for me," Tiffany replied.

"Yes, coffee's fine," Les agreed.

"I'll be right back with fresh coffee. Until then, make yourselves comfortable," Luke said as he headed out the door.

Les took a seat at the conference table and opened his briefcase while Tiffany stared over the river. She and Les were not on the same page. The estate planning process had driven a wedge between them. She wondered why Les had been so difficult.

Les and Tiffany were the sole proprietors of Consolidated Electronics, a 25-million-dollar components company founded by Les's grandfather in 1950. His father gave the company a national profile with circuit protection products. Les was able to take it global when he introduced a semiconductor prototype. Since 2005, the company had been getting stronger and stronger. Government contracts seemed to be showing up at their front door nonstop.

Always an overachiever, Les set the bar high at an early age. Being a star tight end on the football team at Alabama had helped open huge doors for him. Where Les grew up, football wasn't the number one thing—it was more like the *only* thing. Stardom helped athletes advance in business.

Tiffany had been well known on campus too as president of Tri Delta, a cheerleader for the Crimson Tide, and a frequent finalist in beauty pageants. The talented speech major began dating Les in her junior year, and the two of them married right after college. Tiffany proved to be a great asset for Les, especially in the early years. Whenever it was necessary to put his best foot forward at perfunctory "meet and greets," Tiffany stood tall at his side.

Together the power couple attracted some of the best talent in the industry. Funding came easily, and the company experienced 15 years of exponential growth. Tiffany had enjoyed being active in the business, but once the children arrived her priorities changed. Those three children were her main concern as they formulated their estate plan. As she watched Les looking over the final documents, she wondered how he could be so cold toward the children he claimed to love.

"Les," Tiffany said softly as she took her seat next to him. "I have a question before Jim comes in."

"Yes?" Les answered without looking up.

"Are you sure we shouldn't leave the children more?" A hint of frustration tinged her voice. "We've never made big decisions like this unless we're in agreement, but for some reason you're barreling ahead like I don't exist. For a guy that's been so generous, I can't believe you can be stingy toward your own children. Don't you care if they make it?"

Les closed his folder and took a deep breath. This drama was two years running, and just when he thought they were pretty close to being like-minded, Tiffany would return with another appeal. The bickering had taken a toll on their relationship, and he hoped that after today Tiffany would finally let it rest. Apparently his sentimental wife had other plans.

"So what is it now, Tiffany? What do I need to add this time?" Les asked somewhat resigned as he reopened his folder.

"What about emergencies, Les?" Tiffany pleaded. "What will the kids have to fall back on if something happens to the company?"

"Tiffany, they'll each have access to 5 million dollars! That's five times what I wanted to leave them. They need to prepare for their own emergencies. And if they can't figure that out by now, you and I certainly can't help them."

"Les, your father left you the entire company when he died. Where would we be if Papa Shuler had been greedy?" Tiffany said with emotion.

Les was cut to the quick. "It's different today, honey," Les said with a concerned look. "My father left his only child a company with good ideas, average cash flow, and a few national accounts. But I also inherited a complacent labor force and four aging locations with outdated equipment. We weren't on Easy Street! Why do you think we had to go out and raise the venture capital we did?"

"And look what you've done with it since, Les!" Tiffany responded. "You've taken the company way past what your Dad had done by himself. Imagine where our three children could take this! I think the more we leave them, the better."

"The kids get a total of $15 million dollars!" Les answered back. "I think that's enough."

Les had wanted things to be different. God had blessed them

with three healthy and talented children, and he was sure one of them would want to be involved in the business. All along he'd given them opportunities to show their interest. But other than part-time jobs with the company during high school and projects between college careers and trips abroad, none of the three showed the level of commitment Les was looking for in the next owner of the company. All of them loved what the company provided, but none of them wanted to give back.

Their oldest son, Chip, was as different from his dad as he could be. He wasn't athletic, and after four years of struggling through business courses at the local community college, his associates degree was still nowhere in sight. His current set of friends didn't help him a bit. Responsibility was a foreign concept to them. Chip was a good kid, but he'd definitely need some financial help if he kept drifting down his current path.

Brittany had the strengths of both parents. She had drop-dead looks and a brain to match. Following in her mother's footsteps, she gracefully handled being the center of attention. After graduating with a degree in communications, she had moved quickly from intern to assistant director of Corporate Communications at Consolidated. Les was glad she had a high-paying job with the company, and although at some point she might be able to run the entire operation, that was at least a decade away.

Steve, their third child, was hard to figure. Just entering his senior year at Alabama, he wavered between the ministry and the medical field. A solid academic performer with excellent discipline, Steve also possessed a servant's heart. At this point in his life he was sure of one thing: He wanted to work directly with people. He wanted to count.

Les would do anything for his children, but he required them to do their part. Tiffany tried to do everything for them. She didn't consider them to have "a part."

No wonder when it came time to plan their estate, Les and Tiffany's differing parenting philosophies had surfaced again.

The meeting with Mr. Dean was a short one. Within 20 minutes the documents were all signed, and the couple was on their way home. It was a silent ride. Tiffany rode facing the window. In her mind the children had lost. Les looked straight ahead. Hopefully, after today, he and Tiffany could put this behind them. He was anxious to return to a normal life.

Les dropped his wife off at home. On his drive back to the office, he tried to rationalize how this day would play out. He knew he had compromised some when it came to their estate, but he was proud of himself for not giving the children the entire company. Sure, he felt they should have had less, and he worried they still had given them too much. But all in all, Les felt good about the day. As he eased his Mercedes into his reserved parking spot, he couldn't help thinking, *Despite the challenges, life is good!*

Les was walking up to his office when his cell phone rang. He smiled as he read the name on the screen. It was Doc Brown, his personal physician and golfing buddy. Les had put in a call earlier to schedule some golf. Now he wouldn't be playing telephone tag to set the tee time.

Some things will stop a man dead in his tracks. Doc Brown's opening sentence did just that. "Les," Doc Brown began, "you should probably take this call when you get into your office."

Four Years Later

It had been two years since Les passed away. His brave fight with brain cancer bought him an extra six months over Doc Brown's prognosis. Up until the end, Les worked with a divided heart. Tiffany wanted him to do what he could to increase the value of the business. After all, they still had stock in the company. It wasn't the way he wanted it to end.

A few months before Les's death, the final bequests were put in place. But as they had driven home from the lawyer's office, Tiffany wasn't nearly as confident as she had been two years earlier when they had first met with their attorney. They did revise their wills to leave the kids more than they had the first time. They would never have to work another day in their lives, but suddenly that really didn't seem all that important.

Tiffany had been the first to speak that day. "Les, I want you to know how proud I am of you. You've truly fought the good fight of faith these past two years. I can't imagine life without you. I'm sorry I've been so focused on how much our kids will have one day. I think I've missed what they've had all along."

"We all make mistakes," Les responded. "I tried to tell you *how much* wasn't nearly as important as *should we?* I feel bad enough leaving my children without a father. God knows they still need guidance. Knowing I'm not long for this world, the last thing I wanted was for them to worry about money. So I think increasing their inheritance was the right thing."

"Do you really think so?" Tiffany asked. "I've always thought that the more the children inherit, the better off they will be."

⚅

You and I may never own a company like Consolidated Electronics, but that doesn't keep us from thinking like Tiffany and Les. Both wanted their children to have more than they had starting out. Les did his duty and provided. Tiffany got her wish to leave the kids more. And their children certainly were "fixed for life" financially. But was that noble dream the best one?

Les's intuition early on was right. The real issue was never "how much" but "should" they? With all of the focus on leaving their children the financial capital they'd need to succeed, they failed to consider the condition of their kids' spiritual and social capital accounts.

**THE LIE: "The more my children inherit,
the better off they'll be."**

I remember vividly a gentleman I met who had stopped in Atlanta on his way to Florida from a northern state. He had contacted our office and indicated he wanted to visit about estate-planning issues. I met him for breakfast. As he relayed his story, it broke my heart to hear him lament that he'd amassed 10 million dollars but didn't really know his children. He was in a quandary because he felt he couldn't leave his money to them because it would do further damage to their lives. As tears streamed down his face, he expressed his great regret in not focusing on a "wisdom transfer to his posterity" (his children). I wish this was an isolated story, but unfortunately in my 30-plus years it's been a common refrain. Like Les and Tiffany, many parents focus on giving their children money, but in so doing they often fail to give them the necessary wisdom for successful and happy lives.

THE TRUTH: "Wisdom along with an inheritance is good and an advantage to those who see the sun. For wisdom is protection just as money is protection, but the advantage of knowledge is that wisdom preserves the lives of its possessors" (Ecclesiastes 7:11-12).

The truth that's so clear in these verses from Ecclesiastes is that both wisdom and money can provide protection, but only one—wisdom—can preserve the life of its possessor. Wisdom is "the application of biblical knowledge in a practical and successful way." So how do we leave wisdom to our children? I want to focus on two high-level ways that we can pass on wisdom, thus implementing the truth of these verses. There are other ways, but these are undoubtedly the big two. For a more detailed treatment of these concepts, I encourage you to read Ron Blue's book *Splitting Heirs* and my book *Your Life... Well Spent.*

Proper upbringing is the ultimate
safeguard against the problems
inherited money can create.

Spend Time with Your Children

I've watched people spend their entire lives amassing a lot of money so they can give their children all the things they didn't have. But what their kids *really needed* was more of *them* and less of their money. As one person put it, "My dad likes to say that he was home every weekend, and I have no reason to doubt him. But he was never there for me mentally or emotionally. There was no direction, no advice, just money."[1]

Spending time with our children is the only way to really teach them the traits they need to live productive and positive lives. Money can't do it. Money cannot replace the training time necessary to pass on good character. Many benefactors have come to realize that proper upbringing is the ultimate safeguard against the problems inherited money can create. As Tim Kimmel says, "You cannot leave character in a trust account. You can't write your values into the will. You can't bank traits like courage, honesty, and compassion in a safe-deposit box. What folks need is a plan—a long-term strategy to convey their convictions to the next generation." The only way to do that is to spend time with your children and have an intentional plan to train them.

Deuteronomy 6:6-8 spells this out when it says we're to teach and train our children as we sit, walk, lie down, and rise up. You've heard it said that more is *caught* than *taught*. How can our children catch our values and learn how to live the best lives if we're never around to model how to do it? Like Clarence Budington Kelland said, "Dad didn't tell me how to live; he lived, and let me watch him do it."

Since Julie and I were fortunate to observe many situations like Les and Tiffany's, we decided early on we would focus on building social[2] and spiritual capital[3] simultaneously with building our financial capital.[4] And if push came to shove, we would err on the side of time with our children versus putting more money in our bank account. We developed a list of capital development items we wanted to instill in our boys before they left home. ("Institute of Capital Development" in the appendix offers a snapshot of what this list might look like.) Then we did our best to help the boys advance in those areas.

As parents, we should be more interested in seeing positive character traits developed in our children than skill areas, such as music or sports. We're quick to make sure our children get the best instruction in how to hit or shoot or throw a ball, do the proper dance moves, perform the correct gymnastic flips, or play a musical instrument well, but so many times we neglect actively working on the character-building part. As family psychologist John Rosemond points out, "If their children grow up with lots of different skills but lack strength of character and family values, their skills won't amount to a hill of beans. It's character that makes the difference in life."[5]

Expect Your Children to Work

Many of the character traits we want our children to learn to help them manage any money we may leave them are developed as a result of working. When I speak on this topic I always ask, "What is the worst thing that can happen to your children if you don't leave them a lot of money?" Invariably the answer is, "They will have to work like I did." And I then say, "So they can develop the character qualities you've developed?" This creates a sort of "aha" moment as the realization of what this might mean regarding our desire to accumulate assets to leave to our children sinks in.

Parents, no matter how wealthy they are,
should make sure their children work.

Anna Laetitia Barbauld, a Christian writer from the 1700s, stated, "You that have toiled during youth, to set your son upon higher ground, and to enable him to begin where you left off, do not expect that son to be what you were—diligent, modest, active, simple in his tastes, fertile in resources…poverty educated you; wealth will educate him. You cannot suppose the result will be the same."

This is a sobering reminder that it really does make little sense for us to overwork so we can indulge our children. I frequently told my boys that I wanted them to have the experiences I had growing up—and that meant having it tough in comparison to many of their friends. I didn't want to give them too much too soon because I didn't want to deprive them of the privilege of working, nor did I want to undermine their character development. Admittedly they weren't too excited at the time, but as they've started their own careers they've thanked me.

Parents, no matter how wealthy they are, should make sure their children work. David Rockefeller Jr., whose extended family still holds biannual meetings at which 50 to 100 Rockefeller kin turn up, says, "The most important thing we can do is to help give our children a sense of confidence in who they are, their own abilities. That's what will sustain them even if they are wiped out in the stock market tomorrow."[6] Billionaire Warren Buffett says, "My kids are going to carve out their own place in this world, and they know I'm for them whatever they want to do." But he also believes that setting up his heirs with a "lifetime supply of food stamps just because they came out of the right womb" can be harmful for them and is an antisocial act.[7]

Psychiatrists say the lack of work experience only alienates heirs from everyday people and contributes to insecurity about their ability to survive. T. Boone Pickens, a Texas billionaire states, "If your kids grow up living in fairyland thinking that they're princes and princesses, you're going to curse their lives. If you don't watch out, you can set up a situation where a child never has the pleasure of bringing home a paycheck."[8]

As we've moved from an agrarian to an urban society, it's become somewhat more difficult to create an environment for our children to work. I know I experienced this with my boys. When I grew up it was no problem to learn to work. There were plenty of chores for kids to do, including milking cows; feeding sheep, cattle, and pigs; and gathering eggs. During the summers we were on tractors or combines from sunup to sundown. A farmer's work is never done, and typically the whole family is involved. Industrialization and city living makes for a different climate of finding work for kids. I can't send my boys outside to plow a field, pick up hay, or run an errand. I go off to work and can't really involve them in what I'm doing vocationally. Like most children, they're left at home.

The key is that Julie and I knew we needed to do something to train them. And if we have the right objective of teaching our children to work, God will give us wisdom as to what that should look like for our families. It may be yard service, selling magazines door to door, babysitting, doing housecleaning, washing cars, working at the local pool, being an extra hand at a neighbor's construction company. The possibilities are endless, but I've observed that if we're not intentional, the training probably won't happen.

Teaching our children to work will put them in a position to handle wisely any money they may inherit from us.

For our kids I didn't want this to be just "Dad making life rough." I wanted to make deposits into their social and financial capital buckets. I told them I would match them dollar for dollar (up to $15,000) for purchasing a car if they qualified for the Hope Scholarship (a scholarship in Georgia that required a certain high school grade point average). This motivated them to work, save, and keep up their grades. I didn't need to keep after them to find a job or nag about their homework. They were very creative in what they did for income. Sometimes it was mowing yards and aerating lawns. Other times it was putting up and taking down Christmas lights for neighbors or working at a local fast-food place. Now that they're out of college, I'm pleased they've found jobs and are keeping those jobs during these downsizing years. They are good workers, and I know they feel good about providing for their families.

Unlike the gentleman earlier who was afraid to leave his estate to his children, if your children learn to work at least you'll have the viable option of leaving assets to them. The Bible points out the despair that can occur when we labor to amass wealth and then leave it to someone who hasn't labored as well: "I completely despaired of all the fruit of my labor for which I had labored under the sun. When there is a man who has labored with wisdom, knowledge and skill, then he gives his legacy to one who has not labored with them. This too is vanity and a great evil" (Ecclesiastes 2:20-21). Teaching our children to work will put them in a position to handle wisely any money they may inherit from us.

Don't Leave Your Children Too Much

Have you considered how much inheritance you'll leave for your children? Have you wondered how much is enough or even too much? An inheritance that is too much would be any amount that would undermine the development of a solid work ethic and the social capital characteristics that result from working. Also too much would be any amount where there's no need for them to depend on God, which would hinder the development of their spiritual capital base. I think Warren Buffett gave a good perspective on this when he says he wants to leave his children "enough money so that they would feel they could do anything, but not so much that they could do nothing."[9]

Over the years, we've given our clients these general guidelines in drafting their wills depending on their children's ages.

1. *Ages 0 to 20:* Leave enough for education, potentially a house down payment, and potentially enough to get started in a business. The amount shouldn't be so much that they can live off the principal and have no need to work. Remember, work is *essential* to their long-term development of wisdom. Obviously this situation implies a parent who dies young, so the inheritance would need to be overseen by someone other than the children (usually in a trust).

2. *Ages 20 to 40:* During this time, it's also a good idea to begin to make smaller lifetime gifts of varying amounts at different times (so they don't expect it). This enables you to observe and discern if they can handle money in a wise manner. *Caution:* Be careful not to evaluate how your children spend and use money through

your grid, i.e., the way you would handle it. All too often parents unfairly evaluate their children's spending habits in comparison to theirs. Every generation is different, and what you're after is to discern if they practice basic stewardship principles, not if they spend just like you did.

I remember years ago being in a client meeting with three generations. Generation 1 complained that Generation 2 spent money on airplane tickets, and that was crazy because they (Generation 1) never flew. Generation 2 complained that Generation 3 spent money on private schools, and that was crazy because they (Generation 2) had not done that.

The issue is whether your children understand and implement the principles of spending less than they make, paying off debt, keeping current with taxes, diversifying, and so forth. Don't evaluate each specific purchase. Many times you might need a third party to help in this evaluation of the next generation because you are too close to be objective. I have a long-time client whom I've had to remind frequently that his son is doing okay. Even though he spends and uses money differently than his father, he is still exhibiting wisdom in how he is handling it.

Here are some tips to help you evaluate adult children's fiscal responsibility:

- Do they spend less than they make?
- Do they have a healthy fear of debt?
- Are they exhibiting generosity?
- Are they good workers? Do they have and maintain jobs?
- Are they teachable? Do they seek counsel and accountability in the financial area?
- Do they exhibit gratitude?

Based on your observation of how they managed their financial gifts, you can increase or decrease the amount you've left to them in your will.

3. *Ages 40 and over:* By this time you should have a good idea of whether your values have caught on with the next generation. At this point you're typically free to leave an ever-increasing amount to your children without the risk of undermining their self-worth. This assumes they have made it "on their own," as discussed earlier.

The "how much" question is always delicate and complicated. Too much too soon can cause considerable suffering and deprivation because the children will develop little self-respect. It will be hard for them to take much satisfaction in their accomplishments since they will always suspect that their successes are, at least partly, the result of the wealth they have inherited.[10] We counsel our clients that when in doubt, err on the side of less rather than more. After all, the worst thing that can happen is they have to work for a living and develop more character.

Returning to our story about Les and Tiffany. Les intuitively knew the importance of thinking through how much to leave his children. Unfortunately his health situation caused him to err on the side of more versus less. Their wealth gave them the opportunity to fund the lie that the more they left their children, the better off their children would be. If you're reading this chapter and you're just barely making it financially…and if estate planning is the furthest thing from your mind—count your blessings! You may be better off than you think. You don't have to worry about leaving too much to your children and potentially undermining their work ethic development. This chapter's money lie currently isn't an issue for you. Your children will have to work and develop some of the positive character traits we have discussed.

We counsel our clients that when in doubt,
err on the side of less rather than more.

If you have been blessed financially, be on guard. You are in a position where it may be difficult to make sure that your children gain wisdom along with their inheritance (Ecclesiastes 7:11-12).

Stay in balance. Don't accumulate to give your kids more and more. Focus on building their social and spiritual capital so the "how much" question will become easier to answer.

◄ THINKING IT THROUGH ►

❏ Why do you tend to indulge your children?

❏ What do you think about the "less versus more" concept?

❏ Have your children learned how to work?

❏ Do you and your spouse (if married) know what your children will inherit?

❏ Do you have a will?

14

VIEW FROM THE TOP

As the long, black limo made its way under the hotel canopy, a cold Chicago rain continued to fall. Exiting quickly, the cheerful driver turned to two waiting men.

"Good evening, gentlemen. Preston party, I assume?"

"That's us, driver," Vance Preston answered.

"Great!" the driver responded, opening the door. "I'm Fredrick and I'll be taking care of you tonight. We'll be arriving at Tower Place in about 30 minutes. Let me know if you need anything on the way. In the meantime, gentlemen, enjoy the ride."

"Thanks, Fredrick," Vance replied, motioning for Brian to climb in. "We'll be just fine."

Brian quickly slid across the bench backseat.

Vance watched as his wide-eyed assistant took in his new surroundings. *He's like a kid in a candy store,* he thought. "You all right, Brian?" Vance asked jokingly. "You look a little taken aback."

"I'm fine, Mr. Preston!" Brian beamed. "I've never been in a limo before. This thing is amazing! Check out this leather. I bet five cows gave their lives for this ride. And look at the room! You could put the Chicago Bears' front line in here with no problem."

Adjusting his mirror, Fredrick chimed in, "We've done just that, son!"

"I'm not surprised!" Brian shot back. "And check out this bar! Is that for us?"

"Only if you're 21!" Fredrick chuckled.

Turning to his boss, Brian became serious. "Thanks for inviting me to come with you, Mr. Preston. I don't know what to say. This is really special. I want you to know how much I appreciate being here. I'll never forget this."

Pouring himself a drink, Vance Preston smiled politely. In a lot of ways, Brian reminded him of his younger days—aggressive, driven, talented, focused with an eye on climbing the ladder quickly. Raising his glass to his young assistant, Vance said, "Welcome to the top, my man. Welcome to the top." Then he turned and gazed out the window.

Brian watched his boss intently as the limo rolled through the brisk Chicago night. He wondered what it was like to be that successful. His boss had everything. Brian wondered if he had what it took to make it like Mr. Preston had. He wanted to ask more questions of his mentor, but Vance remained exceptionally quiet. After 20 long minutes, the curious assistant had to speak up.

"Mr. Preston," Brian began nervously, "may I ask you something?"

"Sure, Brian," Vance replied without turning around. "What's on your mind?"

"Well, for the past 20 minutes you haven't said a word and... Well, I hate to interrupt your thoughts, sir, but I'm just dying to know what you think."

"Think about what, Brian?" Vance answered, a little surprised.

"Come on, boss. You know! What do you think about the

possibility of taking the President's Award tonight? Do you think you'll win it? It's the most prestigious award the company gives out!"

"Oh, the award." Vance turned and took a sip of his drink. "History's proven that when it comes to winning that award, we never know who'll take it. Besides, Brian, our company has a lot of people who did well this year. There's plenty of competition. But if I say so myself, I think I have a really good chance to win."

"Well, Mr. Preston, I don't know much about the competition, but I do know a few things about you." Brian continued, "For starters, sir, I doubt if you'd be dressed to kill if you thought you'd lose. Look at you. You could stand in a Brooks Brothers' window in that suit!"

"Thanks, Brian. And to be honest with you, that's why I bought this suit—and paid $2500 for it. I felt I needed to look presidential—look the part, if you know what I mean!"

"Well, you sure nailed that. Just like you nailed the Freeman Project. It was dead in the water until they called you in. Then all of a sudden, bang! You turned it around seemingly overnight. How did you do that?"

"Well, I saw a lot of hidden opportunity in that one, Brian. Everyone wanted to bolt when gas prices shot up, but I didn't see the connection. I felt it was still worth the effort. I sensed the market was about to really make a turn in that area," Vance replied with a smile. "And it did."

"I'll say it turned! Not only did we exceed the forecast, the way you handled negotiations with the venture capitalist made the deal even sweeter. Honestly, boss, the way they adjusted their first offer, I was starting to wonder if you didn't have a gun to their heads!"

Peering back out the window again, Vance seemed contemplative. "Sometimes you need to play a little hardball with guys like that, Brian. Truth be told, they wanted that deal as much as we wanted their investment. Once I saw that, I knew we had all the leverage we needed."

"That's precisely what I'm talking about! You see things most people don't. You're amazing, Mr. Preston. You get more done than any three men in the firm, and you don't even break a sweat. I want to be able to do what you do. Will you teach me to do that?"

"I can try, but I have to tell you that when it comes to making deals, it takes sort of a sixth sense," Vance replied, looking back at his assistant. "You either have it or you don't. I guess I have it. It's as simple as that."

"Well, you sure have it!" Brian grinned. "That's why I have no doubt that you'll take the award going away. No one in our company has come close to accomplishing what you've done this year or in the past five years. Not only have you made incredible deals, you've made the company a small fortune! Really, Mr. Preston, can you think of anyone who deserves to get more credit than you?"

Vance Preston thought for a long moment. Then looking his assistant right in the eye, he smiled and raised his glass. "Honestly, Brian, I don't know if I can!"

<hr />

THE LIE: "My talents and abilities produced my wealth."

Vance Preston did what a lot of us do. He drew a straight line between abilities and accomplishments and saw himself standing at the top. In Vance's mind, whatever success he had began and ended with him.

Connecting those dots is easy to do. Let's face it, when we're the center of our world, it makes perfect sense. We get an idea. We work hard to make it happen. Why should anyone else get the credit? And if our own thinking isn't enough to convince us of our merit, the world applauds the "self-made man." He's affirmed and put on a pedestal just like Mr. Preston was. The adjective "success" sticks to our names. As a result, it's logical for us to take credit for what we have. But that's a lie, and it results in arrogance and pride.

> THE TRUTH: "You may say to yourself, 'my power and my own ability have gained this wealth for me,' but remember that the LORD your God gives you the power to gain wealth, in order to confirm His covenant He swore to your fathers, as it is today" (Deuteronomy 8:17-18 HCSB).

One amazing characteristic of the Word of God is its supernatural ability to "judge the thoughts and intentions of the heart" (Hebrews 4:12). In a very real way, the Word corrects our faulty thinking. This faulty thinking can show itself in a number of ways, but one clear manifestation is found in the way we talk to ourselves. This verse hits our misguided self-talk head-on.

All our increase and provision can
be traced back to God's hand.

All of us talk to ourselves, and God knows that. And when we do, we tend to either talk ourselves up or talk ourselves down. Either way, in His infinite wisdom God knows exactly how the conversation will go. So right off the bat He cautions us *not* to draw the same line Vance Preston did. Instead, when we enjoy success, we are to pause and remember that God's power was at work all along the way. If we're going to talk to ourselves, we should be reminding ourselves how God ordered our lives!

The accumulation of wealth or the size of our paychecks doesn't necessarily affirm our abilities. It simply confirms God's covenantal promise to provide for our needs. And He's able to do that creatively in each of us—many times above and beyond what we think. All our talents originate with God. All our wealth belongs to Him.

I've been in the financial services business a long time. I have seen individuals who didn't appear to have much talent or ability make large annual incomes and accumulate incredible amounts of wealth. On the other hand, I've worked with people who had great natural abilities, were very well educated, and yet didn't have nearly as much financially. I'm sure you've observed the same in your sphere of influence.

If you analyze the sources of wealth, you soon realize that income and wealth are largely functions of the vocations we choose, which are often based on how God has gifted us, and how His hand is on that vocation.

God has chosen to bless us with unique gifts that enable us to perform with excellence certain vocations during our time here on earth. Those jobs or vocations generate a certain amount of income, and thus a certain level of potential wealth. A teacher will likely never make what a doctor will make. A doctor may never make what a real estate developer will make. So it's healthy to recognize that our ability to gain wealth is primarily a function of the vocation we feel called to. *Our response is to be obedient to God's call and work hard in that call.*

Even more importantly, we need to recognize that regardless of our vocation (teacher, mail carrier, businessperson, doctor), all our increase and provision can be traced back to God's hand. Wealth is not always a function of how hard we work. (We'll cover that lie in the next chapter.) It's purely the result of the providence of God.

My best illustration of the truth that God gives power to make wealth comes from my agrarian background. Consider the farmer. Every farmer does his part, which is to till the land, sow the seed, and fertilize. It is God, however, who causes the growth. A wise farmer never thinks he is going to go out one year and make "X" amount of money off his crops. He knows he's totally dependent on God for both the yield from the fields and the crop price at market time. Unfortunately, as we've moved from an agrarian society to a more urban society, much of that thinking has changed. Now many believe it's all up to us. Our abilities will make the money. We are in control of the process.

In studying the parable of the farmer in Luke 12:16-21, we can gain some critical insights. In those verses it states that it was the *land* of a certain rich man that was productive. It doesn't say anything about the rich man being productive; the land produced his riches. Even though the land produced the increase, this didn't stop the farmer from claiming credit. In verses 17-19, he uses the personal pronoun "I" or "my" 11 times! Isn't that just like us? We're able to make it to the top like Mr. Preston, and then we don't even stop long enough to think that anyone else deserves any credit.

This thinking leads to incredible pride, a trait which is not pleasing to God. We are clearly told this in 1 Peter 5:5: "God is opposed to the proud, but gives grace to the humble." In verse 6 we're told to "humble [ourselves] under the mighty hand of God, that He may exalt [us] at the proper time." Vance Preston should have exhibited an attitude of humility when talking with his assistant instead of arrogance.

Which of us, when taking an honest look back at our lives, can't see how a teacher, a friend's counsel, an unselfish act, or even just "being in the right place at the right time" played a significant part in getting us to where we are today? As I think back on my life, I'm overwhelmed by God's goodness and His work in my life. Sure,

I've been diligent to work hard and have made good decisions, but God has been providentially at work in the background to enable me to be where I am today.

There are two parts to this success equation. The first is *our part.* This is where we recognize our calling and then teach, sell, develop, practice medicine, or do whatever our calling involves. And we are to do it heartily. The second part is to allow God to do *His part.* He produces the income, brings in the clients, allows the next sale, and ultimately provides the income.

Understanding these two parts will enable us to be grateful and humble. As we acknowledge God's provision and remain confident that He will *always* meet our needs, pride will be uprooted from our lives. As we exercise humility while we're working, we will find ourselves more and more thankful and, thus, more pleasing to God.

God is in charge of the results.

The answer Vance should have given Brian could have been twofold. First of all, he should have said, "Yes, Brian, I did work hard. But the real credit for my success goes to God. *He* has blessed me with ability and success. He gets all the credit."

Second, he should have encouraged Brian to focus not on him and being like him but rather on being all God has for him to be— to maximize his God-given talents. If Brian focuses his attention on the Lord and has a *vertical perspective* instead of a horizontal perspective, that will lead him to freedom.

If we try to be like somebody else, we may never measure up. If we seek after the income someone else makes, that will never lead to fulfillment. Brian needs to be encouraged not to focus on end results (such as receiving an award), but to focus on the process of being all that God has called him to be. God is in charge of the results. There is tremendous freedom that results from focusing on the process as opposed to striving to get to the top.

What about you? Are you taking it one day at a time and working on being all that God has called and equipped you to do? That's the key to freedom.

❧ THINKING IT THROUGH ❧

❏ Do you give thanks for the money that comes in?

❏ If yes, how regularly? Be specific: daily, weekly, monthly, annually?

❏ Do you think you are overpaid or underpaid for what you do? Explain.

❏ Are you as grateful for your gifts and talents as you are for the money that comes in because of them? Explain why or why not.

❏ Do you envy the success of others? Does that envy make you less content with your life?

❏ Can you recall a situation where God provided, and you knew it was from His hand and not yours? If yes, what did that teach you?

15

DRIVE TIME

When I (Kelly) met with Russ for financial counsel, it wasn't like taking a class or attending a seminar. In fact, we never once opened a book, studied a spreadsheet, or needed a calculator. We met only twice a year, and rarely did we spend more than an hour together. Yet every one of those meetings affected my life deeply. Here's how those sessions worked.

Russ would start by asking some big picture questions about my business. How much work did I have in the pipeline? How was my cash flow? What was my growth plan? Then he'd ask about our personal finances. What were our living expenses? How did Mary and I handle giving and taxes? What debts did we have? Usually, this took about thirty minutes. Then, no matter where Mary and I were with our finances, Russ would always do two things. He always reminded me that God owned it all. And he always reviewed the five uses of money: living, giving, taxes, debt, and savings.

Normally I would come to our meetings with a particular issue (or problem) on my mind. It could be anything from expanding my business to building a house. Whatever the question, I always assumed that making more money was part of the answer. Surprisingly, Russ never pointed to more money as a solution to anything. He would point me to God's Word. Instead of telling me what to do, he gave me a biblical principle to think on. He said following those principles would lead to good decisions.

When I first met Russ, I firmly believed in the common sense principle that said the harder I worked, the more money I'd make. My plan was to work as hard as I could and make as much as I could. Then once I had enough money, I'd let Russ tell me how to invest it. Then Mary and I could live happily ever after. Sound familiar?

When I shared that long-term strategy with Russ, he simply smiled and said, "Hey, you need to work as hard as you can, but don't ever assume that working harder will guarantee you more money. Ultimately, God determines how much money you make."

Even before his gripping remark, I had a pretty good idea that Russ Crosson wasn't perfect. Now I was sure of it. His comment made no sense whatsoever. Consequently, I didn't go away listening that day. In fact I went away determined to prove just the opposite.

The truth is that the counsel of God isn't just brilliant, it's consistent. You may reject it from one source, but if God wants to get a lesson across to you, He will. And shortly after that meeting with Russ, God found a very creative way to reinforce his words.

I'd agreed to do a small team-building event for a Christian school on the west side of Atlanta. The headmaster was a friend who had asked for my help. This was a new school with a small faculty and a tiny budget. Consequently, my fee was about a third of what I normally charged.

The scheduled day arrived, and I headed for the school. It was a cold and windy January morning with a steady light rain and temperatures just below freezing. It was one of those days that I'd stay home if I could.

Along the way, my lack of detail showed itself. The school was much further away than I thought. As I began to recalculate my arrival time, I noticed that the rain had increased. The traffic was now moving slower and slower. And when the road narrowed from four lanes to two, I felt a knot in the pit of my stomach. This was not looking good at all!

The more the traffic slowed, the more anxiously I tapped the steering wheel. I began to gripe a little under my breath, but that soon gave way to talking out loud. At first my whining was about traffic and weather. Soon it seemed everything else was going wrong. I began thinking about my usual fee and reminded myself that this job only paid one third of that. I wondered (and seriously doubted) if my headmaster friend understood the value he was getting or the tremendous sacrifice I was making for him and his school. No, I was convinced the guy was clueless!

The longer I sat there, the worse this job looked. I wasn't just aggravated; I was angry. My one-man pity party was ramping up. I questioned why I took the job in the first place, and I convinced myself I was actually losing money!

It's God who determines how much money you'll make.

I was in trouble in more ways than one. Not only was I stuck in traffic with a bad attitude, but I was also stuck behind a working garbage truck that was stopping every 50 feet. I was going to be extremely late, and there was nothing I could do about it.

When God wants our attention He can easily get it. And on that particular day, He wanted my attention in a very big way.

As I sat there sinking into a spiritual abyss, something caught my eye. It had probably been there all along, but I really hadn't noticed. Two men would jump off the garbage truck and sprint over to the curb. Working together, they'd drag the big, blue garbage cans back to the truck and onto a lift, which then dumped the garbage into the truck. Then they'd sprint back to the curb with the empty container and make a beeline back to the truck. These men were working hard. Some of the cans had no lids and were full of water from the rain. It took everything they had to drag them to the truck. But they never once stopped or slowed down. Their diligence was amazing. Their attitude was humbling.

I didn't know these men personally. I didn't have to. All I know is what God firmly impressed on my heart that day. *Even with my "incredibly generous discounted rate," I'd probably make more money today than these men would make in a week.*

For the next 40 minutes I didn't take my eyes off those men. It was one of the most embarrassing, convicting, needed moments of my Christian life. And as I watched those two guys work, Russ's words came flooding back: "It's God who determines how much money you'll make."

Right there in front of me was a living illustration of a biblical principle: *There is no correlation between how hard we work and how much we make.* There is a cause and effect, but not a correlation. None. The only explanation for how much we make is not our brilliance or our labor. It's the providence of God and our vocation He inspired.

I was working hard to "get ahead." My plan was to out-earn my needs for a period of time so I'd have enough to quit working. As noble as that sounds, Christians don't go to work to get ahead. The reason we work hard is because God commands us to do so. And work is a place where we get to display Jesus Christ.

Hard work with an attitude of gratitude is one of the most powerful ways to display Christ. The two men working in front of me had smiles on their faces despite the kind of day it was, the kind of job they had, or how much money they made. And that was more than I could say about me. As I thought about these men, I also thought back to how Russ's advice about my problems never focused on my income.

☜

The Lie: "The harder I work, the more money I'll make."

Like Kelly, unfortunately, many people have bought this lie and its logical conclusion: "More money is the solution to all my problems." The result is we lead unbalanced lives as we focus on trying to make more money. We ignore our spouses, family, friends, and even God because we think one more call, one more deal, one more opportunity will give us more dollars. Then we'll rest.

The Truth: "It is vain for you to rise up early, to retire late, to eat the bread of painful labors; for He gives to His beloved even in his sleep" (Psalm 127:2).

What does this mean? As Charles F. Deems once said, "All men must work. But no man should work beyond his physical and intellectual ability, nor beyond the hours which nature allots. No net result of good to the individual or to the race comes of any prolonging of the day at either end...Work when it is day. When night comes, rest."[1]

Russ's Experience

In my early days as a financial advisor, I too bought into this lie and would put in a lot of overtime. I felt the clients I served and my subsequent income were up to me. So I would swing in and out of any semblance of balance. I knew I was getting out of balance when my wife would subtly and gently remind me when I got home the names of my boys: "Russ, this is Clark, your oldest son," she would start. That was her way of saying I hadn't been around the house very much lately. She would then tell me that my clients came from God, that I could trust Him for new business, and I could work my allotted time and go home.

Focus on achieving the "balance of working."

Stepping back, I then realized I had let my life get out of balance. I knew I needed to balance my time among the five key areas of life: my family, my vocation, my church, my community, and my civic responsibilities. (God, of course, is over all five.) The irony was that I was counseling my clients about having financial finish lines and living balanced lives! And here I was falling short of it myself. I needed to focus on achieving the "balance of working."

By now you may be asking, "Isn't hard work a virtue and sloth a vice?" I agree that sloth is not good. I have seen people hide behind "being home" and using their families as an excuse for neglecting work. In reality they're slacking off and cheating their bosses. This, however, is usually the exception. The more serious and prevalent problems are workaholics who lack sensitivity when it comes to their family lives. Like I did, many justify overworking. "If I make more money, I can spend more time with my kids later." "If I work just a little harder, I will be promoted and make more money." This is a vicious cycle and contrary to the way God wired us for balance and rest. (Being out of balance for a *short* time frame may be justified if you are going to school, learning a new job, developing a new skill, or something similar. The operative word is "short.")

What I've Learned About Work

I found that to live the truth of Psalm 127:2, I had to think correctly about my work. I share some of what I learned here, acknowledging that there are many good resources that go into much more depth on this issue of work. Two sources I heartily recommend are *Your Work Matters to God* by Doug Sherman and William Hendricks (NavPress, 1990) and the booklet "Why Go to Work" by the Vision Foundation in Knoxville, Tennessee. So what have I learned?

1. *There is always one more important thing I can do.* It's true! Work always exceeds the time I have. For that reason, I needed some boundaries. For me, it was committing to be home for dinner with the family each night. (If I needed to miss dinner, I discussed it with Julie ahead of time when possible.) There were many days when I left the office with tasks undone or calls to make because I'd made the commitment to be home. Looking back, going home early never caused me to disappoint my clients or miss an important call. Don't let the urgency of work crowd out balance in your life.

2. *Work is ordained and commanded by God* (1 Thessalonians 4:11; 2 Thessalonians 3:10). The first reference says if I'm not working, I'm leading an undisciplined life. The second reference says if I do not work, I am not to eat. What strong encouragement to work!

I don't know about you, but if God commands it, I should be doing it. I didn't want to be considered undisciplined. If that's not enough motivation, then the fact that blessings come from obedience should be. You and I have the same choice in any area of life regarding God's commands. We can obey or not. And He has given us the command to work. In Deuteronomy 11:26-28, it's clear that blessings come from obedience and curses from disobedience. Therefore, I'm motivated to work (versus being lazy and slothful) by obedience. I want to be blessed, not cursed. Unfortunately, people often think that blessings are always financial, but in many cases, the intended blessing may be the ability to sleep, to have a good self-image, to provide for our families, and so on.

3. *Work is good* (Genesis 2:15). Many people consider work bad…a curse…something to avoid. But according to the book of Genesis, God put man in the garden to tend and till it. Work was good. With the fall, however, the *environment* was cursed (Genesis 3:17-19), so work became hard. There were weeds and thistles and all kind of challenges that forced mankind to sweat and toil. It's true to this day. Work is tough, but it remains a good and proper activity. Your boss may not make sense, employees may not do their jobs properly, customers may be too demanding, and there may be a lot of governmental red tape to deal with. Nonetheless, work is *good.*

The frustration we experience as we toil is balanced by the joy of accomplishment and the provisions produced by our work. Once I understood that work was good, I changed my perspective. Rather than overworking to try to make more so I wouldn't need to work, I began to appreciate the process of working. I thanked God for allowing me the privilege to work, which led to even more of an attitude shift and better balance.

4. *Work is really a gift from God.* "Are you kidding me? A gift?" you ask. Yep! Ecclesiastes 5:18-19 says it clearly:

> "Here is what I have seen to be good and fitting: to eat, to drink and enjoy oneself in all one's labor in which he toils under the sun during the few years of his life which God has given him; for this is his reward.

Furthermore, as for every man to whom God has given riches and wealth, He has also empowered him to eat from them and to receive his reward and rejoice in his labor; this is the *gift* of God."

God has empowered me to work and to enjoy myself as I labor and toil. This perspective helps me to once again quit trying to get out of work. Instead, I work my allotted time and go home.

5. *Work provides true fulfillment because I'm doing what God created me to do.* This is why retirement to a life of leisure is dangerous—it removes the opportunity of fulfillment that the process of working provides. I remember early in my career meeting with an investment banker from Chicago. He explained how he couldn't understand why multimillionaire business owners who sold their businesses would end up buying another business and going back to work. He shared that during the first few years after the sale, the former owner invested conservatively, three to four years later he'd end up investing more aggressively, and usually by the fifth year he had bought another business and started to run it.

We're never fulfilled just looking
at a pile of investment money.

I told him I understood very clearly why. It's because God created man to work, and that man receives fulfillment from working. We're never fulfilled just looking at a pile of investment money and trying to figure out how to entertain ourselves. Once I understood this, I realized again how senseless it was to attempt to make a lot of money to not have to work. Managing money will not create the fulfillment that the process of working does.

6. *Work provides an environment for living the Christian life, sharing my faith in Christ, and growing with other believers.* Christianity shouldn't be just a segment of our lives; it should overflow into every aspect—especially into our work. Our greater purpose as we work is not primarily to make money, but to share Christ, to grow as believers, to provide for our needs and the needs of others.

7. *A vertical focus in my work produces benefits.* A vertical focus versus a horizontal focus produced two benefits. The first benefit is that I was freed from competition. One of the reasons we are tempted to overwork is because we're looking horizontally— trying to advance or excel over a coworker, to be number one, or to climb the ladder of success. Those things may happen, but they shouldn't be our goal. Our goal is to work with professionalism, integrity, excellence, and a desire to please God. If we do that, the results will take care of themselves. God knows your motives. He is concerned about your attitude, not the results of your labor. I'm a very competitive person by nature, so living the truth of setting boundaries around work (Psalm 127:2) was a challenge. How could I go home before anyone else? They might get ahead of me! Once I realized I was *working to please God* instead of trying to get ahead of a fellow advisor with more new clients or more revenue, I was able to achieve more balance.

The second benefit from a vertical perspective was the realization that *God was meeting my needs—not my job.* Rarely did the biggest clients come from my efforts. As I look back over our firm's history, I'm amused by how we got some of our most important clients. Some came from reading one of our books; others came from referrals by people who knew about our firm but didn't even use our services. I remember vividly early in my career when I received a call from my assistant while I was out of town. It seemed she had received a call from a gentleman "out of the blue" (we know it was from God). He became one of our biggest clients.

Rarely did our efforts produce the number of clients we thought they should.

🎵

These things I've learned about work have freed me to spend more time with people—to talk, to listen, to be sensitive to their needs and spiritual condition. My focus isn't on worrying about clients, the next deal, my income, and so forth.

> Work is simply an environment to
> live and share the Christian life.

I'm sorry to say that early in my career I was known for my insensitivity. Even my locomotion and pace in the office communicated a "get out of my way, I have work to do" attitude. Slowing down to fully engage with people didn't seem to allow me to meet my needs at that time. How wrong I was. God promised to meet my needs, and He has been faithful to do that for these many years. He'll be faithful to do that with you too! Our job is to work heartily with balance, realizing God will meet our needs. This realization, more than any other, made the application of Psalm 127 a reality in my life. God truly is in charge!

If we view work simply as a means to generate income and meet our needs, our lives will be marked by that purpose. We will be *competitive, anxious, unsatisfied, self-centered wealth seekers,* always measuring what we do by the size of our paychecks. On the other hand, if we accept the philosophy that work is simply an environment to live and share the Christian life, confident that God will meet our needs, we will experience freedom, focus on the needs of others, realize that wealth is a by-product not a goal, develop a good self-image, be secure in God, and experience a balanced lifestyle that includes leisure.

I've always liked the following anonymous quote:

> Did you ever see a tombstone with a dollar sign on it? Neither did I. I have known hundreds of men who lived as though their only ambition was to accumulate it, but I have never known one who wanted a final judgment of himself to be based on what he got. A man wants people to read in his obituary, not a balance sheet of his wealth but a story of his service to humanity.

So how do we determine if we're working too hard? How do we make sure we will get the epitaphs we long for on our tombstones?

Look in the Work Mirror

- If you are married, ask your spouse, or if you are single, ask your best friend, "Am I always talking about work, even after I've left the office?"

- Do you own a smart phone? When you're at home or out to dinner with a friend, which takes priority: the relationships of those you're with or an electronic device on your belt? Can you totally ignore it for even a few hours in the evening?

- Can you leave work at the office?

- Can you relax?

- Can you enjoy a vacation without constantly being plugged in?

- Can you sleep? (See Ecclesiastes 5:12.)

- How much of your time do you spend thinking about making more money? Have you convinced yourself that "more" is better?

- Are you anxious?

- How is your self-image? What if your job goes away? Will your self-image still be intact?

- How often do you measure how you're doing by looking at the other guy?

I don't know about you, but these questions went a long way in helping me determine if I was living a balanced life.

These are the lessons I had to learn, and that I helped my coauthor, Kelly, to see clearly. In my office I told him that striving to earn more income wasn't the answer; his income was mostly a function of his vocation, and he was to work hard with the right attitude. As Kelly shared, being stuck behind a garbage truck he saw these truths by observing people with great attitudes working hard even in a downpour.

What about it? Will you trust God to provide the increase? Will you choose to live a life of balance?

❧ THINKING IT THROUGH ❧

❏ How did you do on the "Look in the Work Mirror" questions?

❏ Do you identify with any of Russ's challenges? Why or why not?

❏ Do you believe God meets your needs? Or do you think it is up to you?

❏ Do you see work as a gift from God?

❏ Do you enjoy your work?

CONCLUSION

Thank you for spending time with us. Time is one of the most precious resources you have, and we know you could have chosen to use it differently. We trust you found your investment worthwhile and profitable.

We started out by asking you to do one small thing. We asked you to find your place in the stories we shared. Although many of the characters were fictional, all of the issues in the stories were realistic. They happen every day and probably somewhere in a place near you.

God is greater than he who is in the world.

In areas where your thinking aligns with God's, you probably identified with characters who stood for the truth. In those cases keep it up! In areas where you found your thinking was challenged, we hope you'll seek God's direction regarding your next step to living in financial truth.

People ask, "Where did you come up with these lies?" Without trying to be flippant, we tell them, "We just looked in the mirror." It's not easy to admit, but we too have bought into money lies at one time or another—even when we knew better.

As long as we're on this earth we will continue to be bombarded with lies. Why? Because our enemy, Satan, is prince of this earth and he only has one game. He is a liar, the father of lies, and his lies deceive us (John 8:43-44). Think about that. Lies are all Satan has to work with, and he is really good at it. In fact, he is brilliant. That is the bad news.

The good news? God, who cannot lie, is greater than he who is in the world (Titus 1:2; 1 John 4:4). And He is in us. He is Truth, and His Word contains truth about managing our lives and money. As long as we allow Him to live through us, we will be able to handle anything the world and Satan throw at us (Galatians 2:20). We will be able to distinguish truth from error (lies) (1 John 4:6).

Our challenge to you is to keep seeking God, study His Word (which is the source of all truth), and make it your life goal to think like Him.

Thanks again for allowing us to spend this time with you.

P.S. Please be sure and visit our website at www.truthaboutmoney lies.com

APPENDIXES

LIVING EXPENSES

DATE: _____

	Amount Paid Monthly	Amount Paid Other than Monthly	Total Annual Amount
Housing			
Mortgage/Rent	$_____	$_____	$_____
Insurance	_____	_____	_____
Property taxes	_____	_____	_____
Electricity	_____	_____	_____
Heating	_____	_____	_____
Water	_____	_____	_____
Sanitation	_____	_____	_____
Telephone	_____	_____	_____
Cleaning	_____	_____	_____
Repairs/Maint.	_____	_____	_____
Supplies	_____	_____	_____
Other	_____	_____	_____
Total*	$_____	$_____	$_____
Food*	$_____	$_____	$_____
Clothing*	$_____	$_____	$_____
Transportation			
Insurance	_____	_____	_____
Gas and Oil	_____	_____	_____
Repairs/Maint.	_____	_____	_____
Parking	_____	_____	_____
Other	_____	_____	_____
Total*	$_____	$_____	$_____
Entertainment/Recreation			
Eating Out	_____	_____	_____
Babysitters	_____	_____	_____
Magazines/ Newspapers	_____	_____	_____
Vacation	_____	_____	_____
Clubs/Activities	_____	_____	_____
Other	_____	_____	_____
Total*	$_____	$_____	$_____

	Amount Paid Monthly	Amount Paid Other than Monthly	Total Annual Amount
Medical Expenses			
Insurance	$_____	$_____	$_____
Doctors	_____	_____	_____
Dentists	_____	_____	_____
Drugs	_____	_____	_____
Total*	$_____	$_____	$_____
Insurance			
Life	_____	_____	_____
Disability	_____	_____	_____
Other	_____	_____	_____
Total*	$_____	$_____	$_____
Children			
School Lunches	_____	_____	_____
Allowances	_____	_____	_____
Tuition	_____	_____	_____
Lessons	_____	_____	_____
Other	_____	_____	_____
Total*	$_____	$_____	$_____
Gifts			
Christmas	_____	_____	_____
Birthdays	_____	_____	_____
Anniversary	_____	_____	_____
Other	_____	_____	_____
Total*	$_____	$_____	$_____
Miscellaneous			
Toiletries	_____	_____	_____
Husband: misc.	_____	_____	_____
Wife: misc.	_____	_____	_____
Cleaning/Laundry	_____	_____	_____
Animal Care	_____	_____	_____
Beauty/Barber	_____	_____	_____
Other	_____	_____	_____
Total*	$_____	$_____	$_____
TOTAL LIVING EXPENSES	$_____	$_____	$_____

INSTITUTE OF CAPITAL DEVELOPMENT
"PREPARATION FOR LIFE"

INTELLECTUAL/PHYSICAL

- Music/Art
- Science
- Social Studies/ History
- Mathematics
- English/Language/ Spelling/ Speaking
- Writing
- Reading
- Physical Education
- Foreign Language
- Computer

SOCIAL/EMOTIONAL

- Nutrition/ Eating habits
- Dress
- Manners
- Sexuality
- Financial/ Budgeting (Stewardship)
- Work ethic

- Accepting
- Authority
- Balance
- Bold
- Character
- Compassion
- Courage
- Courteous
- Determination
- Diligence
- Discipline
- Encouraging
- Endurance

- Generosity
- Honesty/Truthful
- Integrity
- Leadership
- Perseverance
- Poise
- Purpose
- Respectful
- Responsibility
- Self-control
- Significance
- Teachability

SPIRITUAL

Basics	Developing Convictions	
- Being sure you are a Christian - Spirit-filled life— loving, kind, patient, forgiving, giving, humble, obedient - Attributes of God - Studying the Bible	- Prayer - Fellowship - Witnessing - Relationship/ Friends - Speech - Adultery - Dating	- Drinking/Smoking - Music/Movies - Work - Money - Homosexuality - Abortion - Divorce

Social Capital Goals

Authority: The power or right to command or act. It is the ability to exercise dominion and control.

> *Measurement:* One understands authority when they exhibit submission to and followership to the one in power.

Balance: An influence or force tending to produce a stable or unchanging system.

> *Measurement:* Not becoming excessive in any area of life.

Bold: Fearless; courageous.

> *Measurement:* Being able to take a stand for God and His Word when needed.

Courteous: Considerate toward others.

> *Measurement:* When thinking of others' needs first comes more natural than thinking of yourself or your needs.

Determination: Firmness of purpose; resoluteness.

> *Measurement:* Keep going with our eyes on God even when faced with troubles or roadblocks.

Encouraging: To give confidence or support to another.

> *Measurement:* Characterized by a kind word or deed done without being prompted by another to do.

Poise: To be balanced; maintain a state of equilibrium.

> *Measurement:* Not easily frustrated or knocked off center.

RECOMMENDED READING

Alcorn, Randy. *Money, Possessions & Eternity* (Wheaton, IL: Tyndale, 2003).

Alcorn, Randy. *The Treasure Principle* (Sisters, OR: Multnomah Publishers, 2001).

Blue, Ron. *Generous Living* (Grand Rapids, MI: Zondervan, 1997).

Crosson, Russ. *Your Life…Well Spent* (Eugene, OR: Harvest House Publishers, 2012).

Stanley, Andy. *Fields of Gold* (Wheaton, IL: Tyndale, 2004).

NOTES

Chapter 4: The Neighbors

1. Thomas J. Stanley and William D. Danko, *The Millionaire Next Door* (Athens, GA: Longstreet Press, Inc., 1996), 7.

Chapter 5: The Dinner Meeting

1. We recommend resources from Crown Financial Ministries, 601 Broad Street, Gainesville, GA, www.crown.org, and Dave Ramsey's Financial Peace University, 720 S. Main St., Clute, TX 77531, www.daveramsey. com.

2. Ibid.

3. David Wills, Terry Parker, Gregory Sperry, *Family. Money.* (Atlanta: The National Christian Foundation, 2008), 7. This book is a free download at http://www.nationalchristian.com/resources/c-books, accessed August 5, 2011.

Chapter 6: The Tipping Point

1. To get more information and check out envelope systems, go to www .mvelopes.com, www.crown.org, or www.daveramsey.com.

2. Arthur Wellington, British soldier and statesman, 1769–1852.

3. Rudyard Kipling, 1865–1936.

Chapter 7: Having It All

1. *USA Today,* February 3, 2011.

2. *The Atlantic,* April 2011.

3. Wayne W. Dyer, *Real Magic: Creating Miracles in Everyday Life* (New York: Quill, 1992), 203.

4. "Mr. and Mrs. Thing," Proverbs 31 Ministries, "radio offer," devotion, Monday, August 8, 2004.

5. *The Atlantic,* April 2011.

Chapter 9: IOU

1. This is not the *marginal tax rate*, which is what we hear about in the news. Marginal rates increase as your income goes up and represents the rate on which the *next* dollar you earn will be taxed.

Chapter 10: Giving It Up

1. C.S. Lewis, *Mere Christianity* (New York: Macmillan Publishing Co., 1952), 118.

Chapter 12: Florida or Bust!

1. This time line adapted from Stephen M. Pollan and Mark Levine, "The Rise and Fall of Retirement," *Worth*, December/January 1995.

2. *Worth*, December/January 1995.

3. *Fortune*, June 24, 1996.

4. *Worth*, December/January 1995.

5. *Fortune*, June 24, 1996.

6. Evan Simonoff, "Grand Illusion," *Financial Planning*, April 1995.

7. *Fortune*, June 24, 1996.

8. Betsy Morris, "The Future of Retirement," *Fortune* magazine, August 19, 1996.

9. Ibid.

10. Pollan and Levine, "Rise and Fall."

11. Ibid.

Chapter 13: Our Best Laid Plans

1. *Fortune*, September 29, 1986.

2. "Social capital" is a resource base that allows one to relate to society. The character qualities necessary for effective and productive interaction in society are part of a person's social capital. For example, responsibility is a necessary trait to hold a steady job, as are punctuality, honesty, integrity, loyalty, discipline, and so forth...Morality is a critical component of social capital and includes ethics, conformity to rules of right conduct, and distinguishing right from wrong. Moral capital or morality flows out of spiritual capital—an understanding of the absolute values of God's Word—and is lived out in the realm of social capital. Consider

the illustration of sex within the context of marriage. One learns from God's Word that sex is only appropriate in marriage (spiritual capital) (Hebrews 13:4). People then live this absolute truth by how they conduct themselves in the social capital area. They relate to the opposite sex in a chaste manner, abstaining from sex until married.

3. "Spiritual capital" or "spiritual resources" includes an understanding of biblical absolutes, of how to come to Christ, of God's character, of how to walk by faith and trust God, as well as biblical principles of money management, child rearing, husband/wife relationships, and other aspects of Christian living. Spiritual capital is knowing the Bible and being able to apply it. It is using the absolute truths of God's Word to determine right from wrong, good from evil.

4. "Financial capital" is money and material assets, including land, stock, and jewelry. If we do not balance all aspects of life early in our vocations, we will miss critical time to invest in the spiritual and social capital of our "posterity" (offspring). Furthermore, the financial capital we have amassed will be for naught if the other forms of capital are not present.

5. "Questions, Answers on 'Frantic Family Syndrome,'" *Pharos-Tribune* (Logansport, Indiana), October 14, 1996, A4.

6. *Forbes,* June 19, 1995

7. Ibid.

8. *Fortune,* September 29, 1986.

9. Ibid.

10. Ibid.

Chapter 15: Drive Time

1. Charles F. Deems, "The Study," 1879, as quoted in Charles Spurgeon, *The Treasury of David,* vol. 3 (Part 2), Psalm 127, under "Explanatory Notes and Quaint Sayings," verse 2, accessed August 3, 2011, www.spurgeon.org/treasury/ps127.htm.